SPECIAL-DAY CALENDAR CARDS

Daisy Day

Creepy Critter Day

St. Patrick's Day

Dr. Seuss's Birthday

Telephone Day

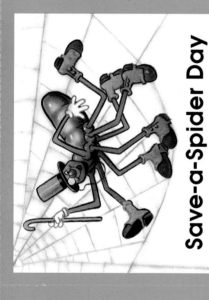

Save-a-Spider Day

Pig Day

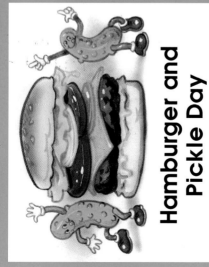

Hamburger and Pickle Day

Pajama Day

SPECIAL-DAY CALENDAR CARDS

Celebrate the Months
MARCH

EDITOR:

Kristine Johnson

ILLUSTRATORS:

Darcy Tom

Jana Travers

Jane Yamada

PROJECT DIRECTOR:

Carolea Williams

CONTRIBUTING WRITERS:

Cindy Barden   Kimberly Jordano

Trisha Callella   Mary Kurth

Rosa Drew   Debbie Martinez

Judy Herz   Terry Petersen

Kathy Hiatt

TABLE OF CONTENTS

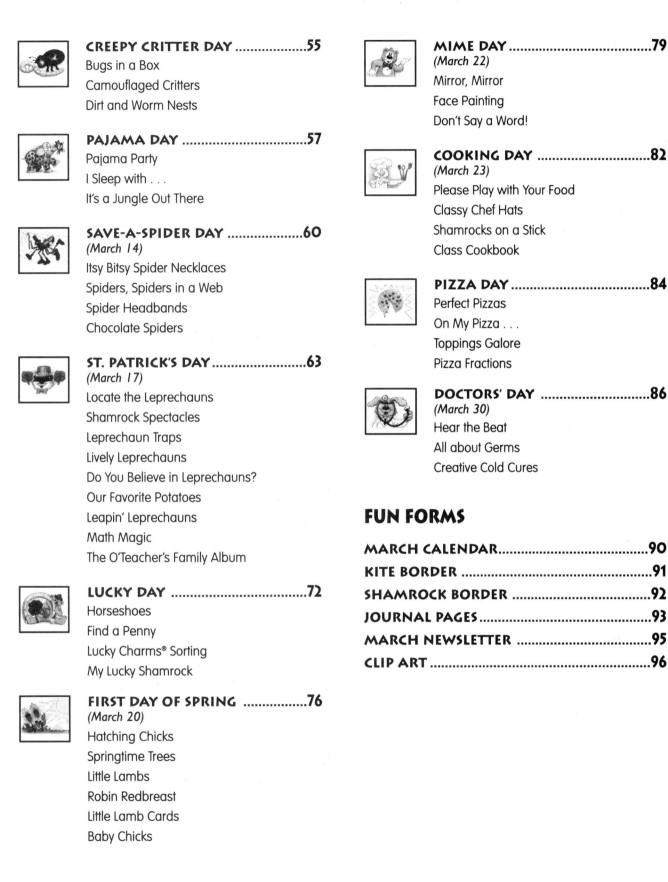

FUN FORMS

INTRODUCTION

Seasons, holidays, annual events, and just-for-fun monthly themes provide fitting frameworks for learning! Celebrate March and its special days with these exciting and unique activities. This activity book of integrated curriculum ideas includes the following:

MONTHLY CELEBRATION THEMES

▲ **monthly celebration activities** that relate to monthlong and weeklong events or themes, such as Lions and Lambs, Drug Awareness Week, and National Nutrition Month.

▲ **literature lists** of fiction and nonfiction books for each monthly celebration.

▲ **bulletin-board displays** that can be used for seasonal decoration and interactive learning-center fun.

▲ **take-home activities** that reinforce what is being taught in school, encourage home–school communication, and help children connect home and school learning.

SPECIAL-DAY THEMES

- **special-day activities** that relate to 15 special March days, including St. Patrick's Day, Save-a-Spider Day, and First Day of Spring. Activities integrate art, songs and chants, language arts, math, science, and social studies.
- **calendar cards** that complement each of the special days and add some extra seasonal fun to your daily calendar time.
- **literature lists** of fiction and nonfiction books for each special day.

FUN FORMS

- a **blank monthly calendar** for writing lesson plans, dates to remember, special events, book titles, new words, and incentives, or for math and calendar activities.
- **seasonal border pages** that add eye-catching appeal to parent notes, homework assignments, letters, certificates, announcements, and bulletins.
- **seasonal journal pages** for students to share thoughts, feelings, stories, or experiences. Reproduce and bind several pages for individual journals, or combine single, completed journal pages to make a class book.
- a **classroom newsletter** for students to report current classroom events and share illustrations, comics, stories, or poems. Reproduce and send completed newsletters home to keep families informed and involved.
- **clip art** to add a seasonal flair to bulletin boards, class projects, charts, and parent notes.

SPECIAL-DAY CALENDAR CARD ACTIVITIES

Below are a variety of ways to introduce special-day calendar cards into your curriculum.

PATTERNING

During daily calendar time, use one of these patterning activities to reinforce students' math skills.

▲ Use special-day calendar cards and your own calendar markers to create a pattern for the month, such as regular day, regular day, special day.

▲ Number special-day cards in advance. Use only even- or odd-numbered special days for patterning. (Create your own "special days" with the blank calendar cards.) Use your own calendar markers to create the other half of the pattern.

▲ At the beginning of the month, attach the special-day cards to the calendar. Use your own calendar markers for patterning. When a special day arrives, invite a student to remove the special-day card and replace it with your calendar marker to continue the pattern.

HIDE AND FIND

On the first day of the month, hide numbered special-day cards around the classroom. Invite students to find them and bring them to the calendar area. Have a student volunteer hang each card in the correct calendar space as you explain the card's significance.

A FESTIVE INTRODUCTION

On the first day of the month, display numbered special-day cards in a festive setting, such as a pot-of-gold display. Invite students, one at a time, to remove a card and attach it to the calendar as you explain its significance.

POCKET-CHART SENTENCE STRIPS

Have the class dictate a sentence to correspond with each special-day card. Write the sentences on individual sentence strips. For example, on St. Patrick's Day you might write *On this special day, we wear green.* Put the sentence strips away. When a special day arrives, place the corresponding strip in a pocket chart next to the calendar. Move a fun "pointer" (such as a shamrock-topped ruler) under the words, and have students read aloud the sentence. On each special day, display the corresponding sentence in the pocket chart.

GUESS WHAT I HAVE

Discuss the special days and give each student a photocopy of one of the special-day cards. (Two or three students may have the same card.) Have students take turns describing their cards without revealing the special days, such as *This is the day we celebrate the birthday of the author of* The Cat in the Hat. Invite the student who guesses Dr. Seuss's Birthday to attach the card to the calendar.

TREAT BAGS

Place each special-day card and a small corresponding treat or prize in a resealable plastic bag. For example, place a chocolate "gold" coin in a bag for St. Patrick's Day. On the first day of the month, pin the bags on a bulletin board near the calendar. Remove the cards from the bags and attach them to the calendar as you discuss each day. When the special day arrives, remove the corresponding bag's contents and discuss them. Choose a student to keep the contents as a special reward.

LITERATURE MATCHUP

Have students sit in two lines facing each other. Provide each member of one group with a special-day card and each member of the other group with books whose subjects match the special-day cards held by the other group. Invite students to match cards and books, come forward in pairs, and introduce the day and book. Display the books near the calendar for students to read.

MINI-BOOKS

Reproduce numbered special-day cards so each student has a set. Have students sequence and staple their cards to make mini-books. Invite students to read their books and take them home to share with family members.

CREATIVE WRITING

Have each student glue a copy of a special-day card to a piece of construction paper. Invite students to write about and illustrate their special days. Have students share their writing. Display the writing near the calendar.

LUNCH SACK GAME

Provide each student with a paper lunch sack, a photocopy of each special-day card, and 15 index cards. Have students decorate the sacks for the month. Invite students to color the special-day cards and write on separate index cards a word or sentence describing each day. Have students place special-day cards and index cards in the sacks. Ask students to trade bags, empty the contents, and match index cards to special-day cards.

SPECIAL-DAY BOX

One week before a special day, provide each student with a photocopied special-day card, an empty check box or shoe box, and a four-page 3" (7.5 cm) square blank book. Ask each student to take the box, book, and card home to prepare a special-day-box presentation. Have students write about their special day on the four book pages and place in the box small pictures or artifacts relating to the day. Ask students to decorate the boxes and glue their special-day cards to the top. Have students bring the completed boxes to school on the special day and give their presentations as an introduction to the day.

NATIONAL NUTRITION MONTH

Relish tasty treats that are also nutritious during National Nutrition Month. Students will learn about nutrition and good eating habits with these scrumptious activities.

Eat Right, Feel Bright

Stomachache	Feeling Great
On Sunday, we ate 1 [chocolate].	On Sunday, we ate 1 🍎.
On Monday, we ate 2 🍩🍩.	On Monday, we ate 2 carrots.
On Tuesday, we ate 3 [chips][chips][chips].	On Tuesday, we ate 3 breadsticks.
On Wednesday, we ate 4 🍦🍦🍦🍦.	On Wednesday, we ate 4 🍌🍌🍌🍌.
On Thursday, we ate 5 🍭🍭🍭🍭🍭.	On Thursday, we ate 5 celery sticks.
On Friday, we ate 6 marshmallows.	On Friday, we ate 6 green beans.
On Saturday, we felt sick.	On Saturday, we felt great!

LITERATURE LINKS

All Through the Week with Cat and Dog,
CTP Learn to Read Series

The Edible Pyramid: Good Eating Every Day
by Loreen Leedy

Good for Me!: All About Food in 32 Bites
by Marilyn Burns

Gregory, the Terrible Eater
by Mitchell Sharmat

Hungry Thing
by Jan Spepian and Ann Seidler

Junk Food—What It Is, What It Does
by Judith S. Seixas

A Piece of Cake by Jill Murphy

Yummers! by James Marshall

EAT RIGHT, FEEL BRIGHT BULLETIN BOARD

With your class, brainstorm and list on chart paper junk foods students eat. On separate sentence strips, write *On Sunday, we ate 1 _____. On Monday, we ate 2 _____. On Tuesday, we ate 3 _____. On Thursday, we ate 4 _____. On Friday, we ate 5 _____. And on Saturday, we felt sick.* Invite students to fill in the blanks with the names of different junk foods from the list or glue junk food wrappers on the blanks to create a fun, fictional story. Attach the sentence strips to one side of a bulletin board titled *Stomachache*. List on the chart paper healthy foods students enjoy eating. Write another set of sentence frames on sentence strips, but on the last one write *On Saturday, we felt great!* Invite students to fill in the blanks with different names of healthy foods or glue on drawings of healthy foods. Attach the sentence strips to the other side of the bulletin board titled *Feeling Great*.

MATERIALS
▲ chart paper
▲ sentence strips
▲ glue
▲ junk food wrappers
▲ drawing paper
▲ crayons or markers

MATERIALS

▲ scissors
▲ paper sacks
▲ egg cartons
▲ film canisters
▲ iodine
▲ eyedropper
▲ food items (regular and light cheese, mayonnaise, pasta, bread, potato chips, salad dressing, fruit, rice, vegetables, nuts, deli meats)

WHAT'S IN OUR FOOD?

Cut paper sacks into 6" (15 cm) squares. Divide the class into small groups and give each group paper-sack squares, an egg carton, a film canister with a small amount of iodine in it, and an eyedropper. Have students place each food item on a separate paper-sack square for five minutes. Ask students to move the food to the egg-carton cups and hold the paper up to the light to check for oily spots. Ask students which items made the paper look and feel greasy. Explain that if the paper feels greasy and has an oily spot, the food contains fat, which comes from oil. Foods fried in oil, such as potato chips and French fries, have a lot of fat. Have groups add a drop of iodine to the food items in the egg-carton cups. Caution students to keep iodine away from their eyes and mouths. Iodine turns bluish black on starchy foods. Explain to students that starch is a carbohydrate, which is a good source of energy. Remind students that they should eat mostly breads, cereals, rice, and pasta, which are rich sources of carbohydrates.

MATERIALS

▲ Nutritious Snacks reproducible (page 13)
▲ craft sticks
▲ paper plates
▲ napkins

SNACK BAR DAYS

Designate every Friday of National Nutrition Month as Snack Bar Day. On this day, make a snack from the Nutritious Snacks reproducible. On the last Friday of the month, invite students to bring in healthy snacks to share with the class.

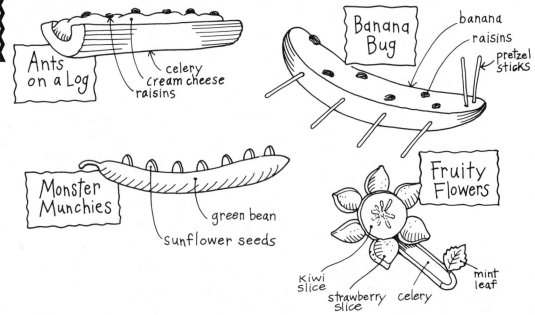

National Nutrition Month

3-D FOOD PYRAMID

Use the Food Pyramid Guide to discuss which foods make a healthy, balanced diet. Ask each student to draw or cut out and glue pictures of food from magazines or coupons inside the corresponding sections of the Food Pyramid reproducible. Divide the class into groups of four and have students cut around the flaps of their triangles, fold the flaps on the dotted lines, and glue the four triangles together to form a three-dimensional pyramid. Discuss how many servings of each food group should be eaten daily for a balanced diet.

HOLD THE FAT, PLEASE!

Label baby food jars *whole, low fat,* and *nonfat.* Pour milk into labeled baby food jars. Add a spoonful of vinegar to each jar and watch the milk and milk fat separate. Pour the mixtures into separate coffee filters. The milk fat will remain in the filters. Ask students to make observations about the different amounts of fat in the three types of milk.

SUPER SUPERMARKET

Divide the class into six groups and assign each a different food group. Have each group draw foods from their food group on folded butcher paper, so when students cut out the food, they will have two copies. Have students color the cutouts, staple them together leaving the top open, stuff them with crumpled newspaper, and staple them closed for a three-dimensional effect. Display the foods in a learning center with a sign that reads *(Teacher)'s Supermarket*. Invite students to use the Food Pyramid Guide to categorize the foods into the food groups, discuss how many servings of each food group are recommended, and create balanced meals with the foods. As an extension, have students write nutritious dinner menus and glue them to the back of paper plates. Invite students to draw their meals on the front of the plates. Hang the plates from the ceiling.

Miss Mallet's Supermarket

FRIENDSHIP FRUIT SALAD

HOME ACTIVITY

Invite students to bring fruit from home in paper sacks. Have students ask adults at home to help them write on the outside of the sack three clues about the fruit. Invite students to read their clues and ask the others to guess the fruit. Divide the class into groups of eight and have them wash, dry, cut, and mix the fruit in a bowl. Have parent volunteers supervise the cutting. Eat and enjoy!

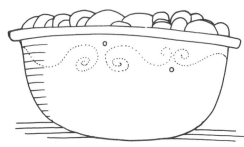

· It grows on trees.
· It's yellow.
· You have to peel it.

Banana Bugs

Ingredients
bananas
pretzel sticks
peanut butter
raisins

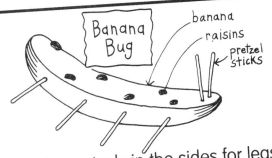

1. Peel a banana and poke pretzels in the sides for legs.
2. Using a craft stick, make spots with the peanut butter.
3. Stick raisins on the peanut butter.
4. Add pretzel "antennae."

Ants on a Log

Ingredients
celery stalks
cream cheese
raisins

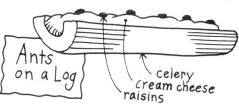

1. Cut celery stalks into thirds.
2. Spread cream cheese in the celery groove.
3. Add raisin "ants."

Monster Munchies

Ingredients
fresh green beans
sunflower seeds
mustard

1. Dab mustard in spots on green beans.
2. Place sunflower seeds on the mustard spots.
3. Dab two mustard eyes at one end.

Fruity Flowers

Ingredients
sliced strawberries
sliced kiwis or bananas
celery stalks
mint leaves

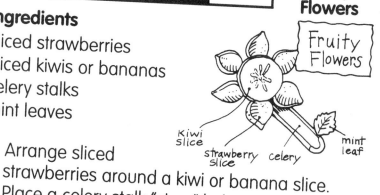

1. Arrange sliced strawberries around a kiwi or banana slice.
2. Place a celery stalk "stem" below.
3. Add two mint leaves to celery.

FOOD PYRAMID GUIDE

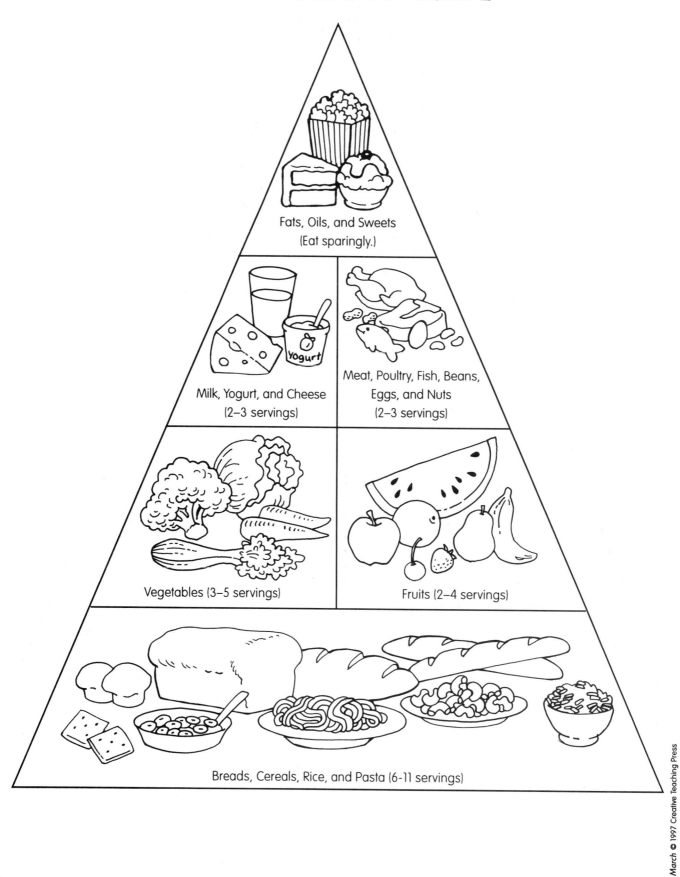

Fats, Oils, and Sweets
(Eat sparingly.)

Milk, Yogurt, and Cheese
(2–3 servings)

Meat, Poultry, Fish, Beans,
Eggs, and Nuts
(2–3 servings)

Vegetables (3–5 servings)

Fruits (2–4 servings)

Breads, Cereals, Rice, and Pasta (6-11 servings)

FOOD PYRAMID

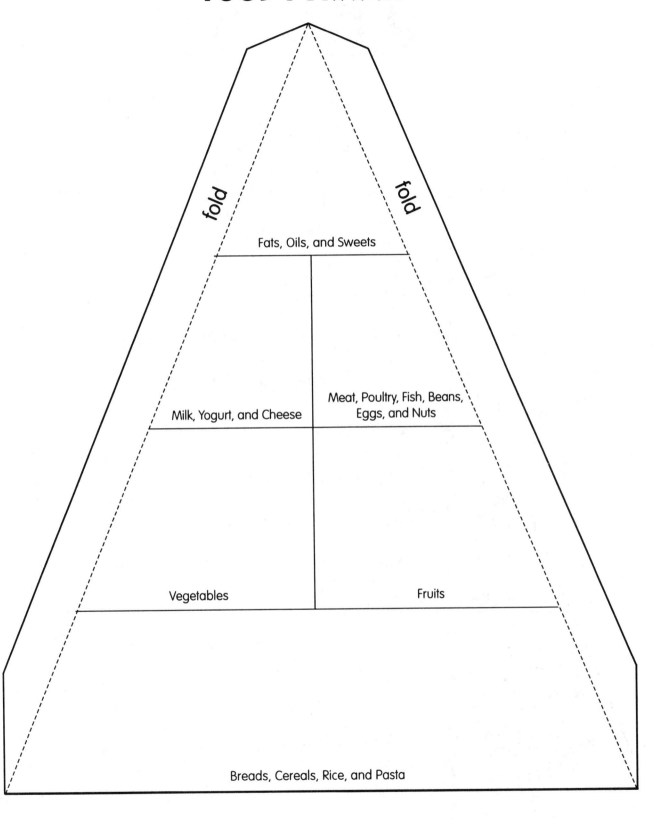

fold

fold

Fats, Oils, and Sweets

Meat, Poultry, Fish, Beans, Eggs, and Nuts

Milk, Yogurt, and Cheese

Vegetables

Fruits

Breads, Cereals, Rice, and Pasta

National Nutrition Month

MERRY MUSIC MONTH

Celebrate Music in Our Schools Month with these toe-tappin' and finger-snappin' activities. They'll be music to your students' ears!

LITERATURE LINKS

Alligators and Music
by Donald Elliott and
Clinton Arrowood

The Bremen Town Musicians
by Hans Wilhelm

The Fabulous Four Skunks
by David Fair

The Happy Hedgehog Band
by Martin Waddell

The Little Band by James Sage

Meet the Orchestra
by Ann Hayes

Music! by Genevieve
Laurencin and Denise Millet

Music, Music for Everyone
by Vera Williams

*The Philharmonic
Gets Dressed*
by Karla Kushkin

*Scott Gustafson's
Animal Orchestra*
by Scott Gustafson

RAGTIME BAND BULLETIN BOARD

Invite students to create instruments, such as flutes, guitars, drums, and maracas from cardboard tubes, shoe boxes, paper lunch sacks, oatmeal containers, and other art supplies. Have students color small paper plates to match their skin color, add facial features, and glue Spanish moss to the top for hair. Attach the faces next to the students' instruments on a bulletin board titled *(Teacher)'s Ragtime Band*. Have students copy and complete on paper strips the frame *(Student's name) plays the (instrument).* Attach the strips below each student's instrument. Sing the following song to the tune of "Down by the Station" and create more verses for each of the instruments in the band.

Down in the classroom,
So early in the morning,
Hear our favorite instruments,
Playing in the band.

Hear the drum go boom, boom.
Hear the flute go tra-la-la.
Boom, boom. Tra-la-la.
All day long.

MATERIALS
▲ cardboard tubes
▲ shoe boxes
▲ paper lunch sacks
▲ oatmeal containers
▲ art supplies (crayons, markers, paint, paint-brushes, yarn, glue, buttons, rubber bands)
▲ small paper plates
▲ Spanish moss
▲ paper strips

MATERIALS

▲ various types of music on tape
▲ tape player
▲ blank journals
▲ crayons

MUSIC APPRECIATION

Gather a variety of music tapes, such as classical, big band, and other instrumental music. Each day of the week play a different type of music as students enter the classroom. Print the name of the musical artist, composer, or type of music on the chalkboard. Have students copy the information in their journals and draw a picture to correspond with the music. Ask students how the music makes them feel. Have students draw or write what they envision while you play a short musical piece. Ask students if the music sounds happy or sad, slow or fast, loud or soft. Invite students to share their interpretations with the class. At the end of the week, play excerpts from different musical pieces and challenge students to identify the type of music.

MATERIALS

▲ kitchen utensils (wooden spoons, cookie sheets, eggbeaters, pots and pans, lids, plastic tubs)
▲ butcher paper
▲ paper towel tubes
▲ masking tape
▲ markers

GADGET BAND

Have each student bring a kitchen utensil to school. (Be sure to have extra "instruments" on hand.) Group instruments into different categories such as plastic tubs in one section, pots and pans in another, and spoons in another. Have each group agree on a symbol for their section of the orchestra, such as a cookie for the cookie sheet section and an egg for the eggbeaters. Tape one end of a piece of butcher paper to a paper towel tube. Invite a member from each group to draw the group's symbol on the paper one after the other. Invite students to take turns drawing until the length of the paper is used up. When the drawings are complete, tape the end to another paper towel tube. Have all the players sit on the floor in their sections. As the conductor, face the group and hold up the score so students can see it. As you slowly unroll one end of the "score," have students play their instruments accordingly. For extra fun, have students play the score backward.

MICHAEL FINNEGAN

(to the tune of "Ten Little Indians")

There was a man named Michael Finnegan.
He grew whiskers on his chinnegan.
The wind came up and blew them in again.
Poor old Michael Finnegan. Begin again!

There was a man named Michael Finnegan.
He went fishing with a pin again.
Caught a fish and dropped it in again.
Poor old Michael Finnegan. Begin again!

There was a man named Michael Finnegan.
He got fat and then got thin again.
Then he died and could not sing again.
Poor old Michael Finnegan. Begin again!

RUBBER BAND INSTRUMENTS

Invite each student to string different sizes of rubber bands over a sturdy open shoe box. Have students pluck the rubber bands. Explain that the sounds the rubber bands make depend on how thick and tight they are. Challenge students to arrange the rubber bands from the lowest to the highest pitch.

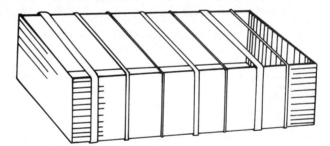

MAKE A LITTLE MUSIC

HOME ACTIVITY

Decorate a canvas bag with music notes and fill it with the Making Music reproducible and a xylophone. Have students take turns taking the bag home to practice playing the songs on the reproducible. Invite each student to share with the class a tune they learned at home.

Dear Family,

We're learning about music at school. I can make music using the xylophone. Please help me color the song notes below to match the colors of the xylophone keys. We can try to make our own song, too. I will get to play one song for the class when I return the bag to school tomorrow. Please help me remember to return the bag and xylophone so another student can take it home.

Name _____

Twinkle, Twinkle, Little Star

C	C	G	G	A	A	G
F	F	E	E	D	D	C
G	G	F	F	E	E	D
G	G	F	F	E	E	D
C	C	G	G	A	A	G
F	F	E	E	D	D	C

Mary Had a Little Lamb

A	G	F	G	A	A	A
G	G	G	A	C	C	
A	G	F	G	A	A	A	A
G	G	A	G	F		

LIONS AND LAMBS

The saying goes, "March comes in like a lion and goes out like a lamb." Engage your students in a rip-roaring lions and lambs weather study. These activities are something to roar about!

LITERATURE LINKS

Dancing with the Wind
by Stanton Orser

Feel the Wind
by Arthur Dorros

Gilberto and the Wind
by Marie H. Ets

How the Wind Plays
by Michael Lipson

Mirandy and Brother Wind
by Jerry Pinkney

One Windy Wednesday
by Phyllis Root

What Makes the Wind
by Laurence Santrey

What's the Weather Like Today?
CTP Learn to Read Series

The Whirlys and the West Wind
by Christine Ross

The Wind Blew
by Pat Hutchins

LION OR LAMB WEATHER BULLETIN BOARD

In advance, color and cut out the Lion and Lamb reproducible. Divide a bulletin board into four or more sections according to the different weather patterns in your area during March. Divide your class into small groups and invite each group to decorate one section of the bulletin board. Each day, have students determine the type of weather, whether it is foul (lion) or fair (lamb) and place either the lion or lamb on the proper section of the bulletin board.

MATERIALS
▲ Lion and Lamb reproducible (page 25)
▲ scissors
▲ crayons or markers

HOLD ONTO YOUR HAT BULLETIN BOARD

Cut out the center of a paper plate for each student. Have students turn paper bowls upside down and slip the paper-plate rings over them so the bowls go through the hole. Have each student glue the bowl rim to the underside of the plate, creating a hat. Invite students to decorate their hats with paint. Write on a bulletin board the poem *Hold onto your hat on a breezy March day or the Old North Wind will blow it away.* Cut out a butcher paper cloud and draw a face on it as if it is blowing. When the hats are dry, display them around the poem.

LION AND LAMB PINWHEELS

Discuss how wind is caused by warm air moving up meeting cool air that is moving down. Have each student color and cut out a Pinwheel pattern. Invite students to assemble the pinwheels and attach each one to a pencil eraser. Take students outdoors to watch how their pinwheels spin to see if it is a lion or lamb day.

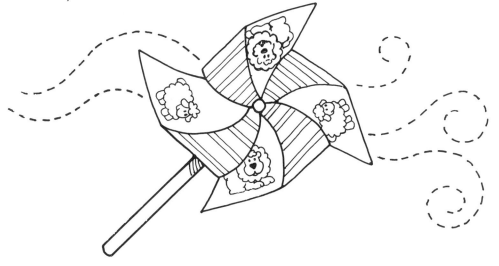

Lions and Lambs

MATERIALS

▲ 12" x 18" (30.5 cm x 46 cm) white construction paper
▲ crayons
▲ diluted tempera paint
▲ straws

WINDBLOWN HAIR

Ask each student to draw a large U shape with marker on white construction paper. Invite students to draw large self-portraits (without hair) using the U shape as a face outline. Place a spoonful of diluted paint (the color of the student's hair) above the forehead on each student's drawing. Invite students to blow through a straw to spread the paint and create windblown hair.

OH, DEAR, WHAT WILL THE WEATHER BE?

At the beginning of the month, invite students to predict how many "lion" (windy or rainy) days and "lamb" (sunny or still) days there will be. Have students record their predictions. Each morning, have a student decide whether it is a lion day or a lamb day and attach a lion or a lamb Calendar Marker to the classroom calendar. At the end of the month, compare the class's predictions with the actual number of lion days and lamb days.

ANIMAL SIMILES

Introduce the concept of similes to your class. (A simile compares two items using *like* or *as*, for example, *quiet as a mouse*.) March weather is commonly compared to a lion and a lamb using a simile. Discuss the different attributes given to lions and lambs. Ask students to each think of three ways they are like lions and three ways they are like lambs. Give each student a blank book. Have students write and illustrate how they are like lions on the first three pages and how they are like lambs on the last three. Hang them on a bulletin board titled *No Lion, This Work Is Grrreat!*

OPPOSITES ATTRACT

Copy and cut out the Calendar Markers reproducible. Write opposite words on index cards, and glue a lion or lamb from the reproducible to the back side of each card. Have students turn the cards facedown and play concentration, choosing a lion and a lamb to match opposites. As an extension, on other cards, write capital and lowercase letters, numerals and number words, rhyming words, or equivalent fractions, and have students match the cards.

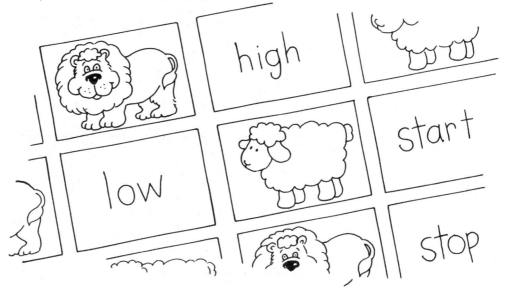

Lions and Lambs

WILD WINDSOCK

MATERIALS

▲ scissors
▲ cardboard oatmeal containers
▲ crayons or markers
▲ glue
▲ construction paper
▲ crepe paper or tissue paper
▲ string
▲ hole punch

Cut out the top and bottom of each cardboard container. Invite students to draw spring scenes on construction paper and glue the drawings around the containers. Next have students cut long streamers from crepe paper or tissue paper and glue them so they hang from the rim of one end of the container. Punch four evenly spaced holes around the rim of the other end of each container. Have students thread string through the holes and double-knot each strand to secure it in place. Tie all four strands together at the top and let students hang their windsocks on tree branches.

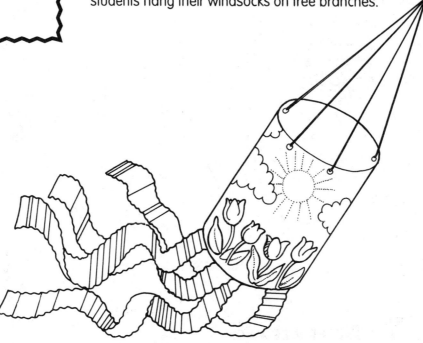

MATERIALS

▲ Emergency Kit reproducible (page 28)

WEATHER EMERGENCY KITS

HOME ACTIVITY

Send home the Emergency Kit reproducible. Explain to students that different seasons can bring natural disasters caused by weather. Have students help their parents put together emergency kits for their homes.

LION AND LAMB

PINWHEEL

1. Color and cut out the pinwheel.
2. Cut on the solid lines.
3. Turn the numbered corners toward the center.
4. Poke a pin through the center of the pinwheel.
5. Attach the pin to a pencil eraser and watch the wind blow!

CALENDAR MARKERS

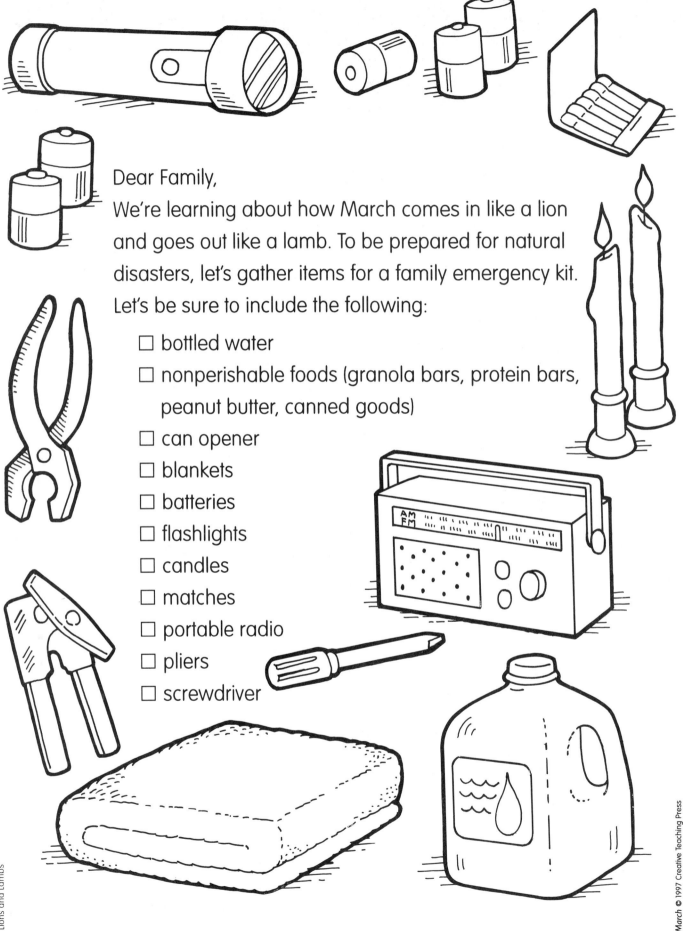

Dear Family,

We're learning about how March comes in like a lion and goes out like a lamb. To be prepared for natural disasters, let's gather items for a family emergency kit. Let's be sure to include the following:

- ☐ bottled water
- ☐ nonperishable foods (granola bars, protein bars, peanut butter, canned goods)
- ☐ can opener
- ☐ blankets
- ☐ batteries
- ☐ flashlights
- ☐ candles
- ☐ matches
- ☐ portable radio
- ☐ pliers
- ☐ screwdriver

DRUG AWARENESS WEEK

National Drug Awareness Week is observed the first week in March. Take this opportunity to discuss with students the consequences of different choices and the dangers of smoking and drug abuse.

LITERATURE LINKS

Alcohol: What It Is, What It Does by Judith S. Seixas

Banana Beer by Carol Carrick

The Berenstain Bear Scouts and the Sinister Smoke Ring by Stan and Jan Berenstain

The Berenstain Bears and the Drug Free Zone by Stan and Jan Berenstain

Cigarettes, Cigarettes: The Dirty Rotten Truth about Tobacco by Pete Traynor

House that Crack Built by Clark Taylor

What Are Drugs? by Gretchen Super

What Would You Do? A Kids' Guide to Tricky and Sticky Situations by Linda Schwartz

HUGS NOT DRUGS BULLETIN BOARD

Discuss some of the dangers of drug abuse. Invite students to write a drug-awareness slogan on the Heart reproducible. Have students cut out the heart shape. Then, invite them to draw a self-portrait, cut it out, and glue it behind the heart. Have students trace their hands, cut out their handprints, and glue them to the sides of the heart, to look as if they are holding it. Students can draw legs and glue them below the heart. Display slogans on a bulletin board titled *Hugs Not Drugs.*

MATERIALS
- Heart reproducible (page 32)
- crayons or markers
- construction paper
- scissors

HEALTHY CHOICES

Cut an opening across the top of two shoe box lids. Label one box *Healthy* and draw a happy face. Label another *Unhealthy* and draw a sad face. Discuss with students different items that would belong in each of these categories. For example, *Healthy* includes eating lots of fruit and vegetables and getting plenty of exercise and rest. *Unhealthy* includes eating too many sugary and fatty foods, drinking alcohol, and smoking. Invite students to work in small groups to cut out magazine pictures of healthy and unhealthy choices and place them in the appropriate boxes. Discuss the choices afterward as a class.

WISE DECISIONS

Using a permanent marker, write the words *Stop, Think, Listen,* and *Decide* on four balloons (one word per balloon). Ask students what decisions are easy for them to make, such as what to eat for breakfast or what to wear to school. Then, ask students what they do if they do not know what decision to make. Tell students you will show them one way to help make wise decisions. Blow up the balloon that says *Stop*. Tell students to give themselves time to think and get advice from others they trust. Blow up the balloon that says *Think*. Tell students to consider if the decision will hurt others or themselves. Blow up the balloon that says *Listen*. Tell students to listen to parents, teachers, or other trusted adults. Blow up the last balloon. Explain that some decisions are harder to make than others and that some have good or bad consequences that could last a long time. Have students role-play to practice facing difficult situations, such as a neighbor offering them a cigarette or a stranger offering them candy.

KEEP YOUR COOL

Ask students to show you a happy face, a sad face, and an angry face. Ask students what they do when they are angry. With your class, brainstorm different healthy ways to handle anger, such as exercising, squeezing a pillow, drawing your feelings, going for a walk or jog, writing a letter, talking to someone, or hugging a pet. Have each student draw a happy face on a paper plate and a sad face on another. Invite students to glue a tongue depressor to the bottom of each plate as a handle. Describe aloud different situations of children dealing with their anger. Ask students to hold up the happy face when the children respond in healthy ways and the sad face when the children respond in unhealthy ways, such as hitting someone, throwing toys, slamming doors, or yelling. After each unhealthy example, help students brainstorm different ways the child could have responded.

PICK-ME-UPS

HOME ACTIVITY

Write *Pick-Me-Ups* on the cover of a blank journal. On the inside front cover write *What could you do to make a friend feel better?* Discuss with students that when people feel sad or sick, there are ways we can help cheer them up. Invite students to take turns bringing home the journal. Send a note home asking family members to discuss with their child the importance of friends and ways they can help others feel good about themselves. Then, have students write what they could do to make a friend feel better, such as sing a song, play a game, make ice-cream floats, give a hug, or hold a hand. Ask students to return the book to school and share their ideas with the class.

Pick-Me-Ups
by Mrs. Williams' first graders

Hi
I could draw a picture to help my friend feel better.

RAINBOWS

Legend says that a pot of gold is buried at the end of every rainbow. Springtime in March is a perfect time to search for rainbows—or make your own. Your students will enjoy colorful days with these activities!

LITERATURE LINKS

How the Sky's Housekeeper Wore Her Scarves
by Patricia Hooper

The Land of Many Colors
by Klamath County YMCA Family Preschool

The Rainbow Fish
by Marcus Pfister

A Rainbow of Friends
by P. K. Hallinan

The Rainbow Goblins
by Ul De Rico

A Rainbow of My Own
by Don Freeman

Raindrops and Rainbows
by Rose Wyler

Skyfire by Frank Asch

Swinging on a Rainbow
by Charles Perkins

A RAINBOW OF WORK BULLETIN BOARD

Sketch on a bulletin board a rainbow outline ending in a pot of gold. Label the pot *A Rainbow of Good Work.* Divide the class into six groups. Invite each group to use different methods of painting to add color to the bands. Have one group sponge-paint red hearts in the top band and another group paint orange pumpkins on the next. Invite another group to press cut potatoes in yellow paint and press them onto the third band to make suns. Have another group paint clover shapes, using green paint, in the fourth band. Invite a group to press their hands in blue paint and press their handprints on the fifth band. The last group can press their thumbs in a purple ink pad to make grapes on the sixth band. After the rainbow is complete, add to the display samples of good student work framed in brightly colored construction paper.

MATERIALS
▲ paint/paintbrushes
▲ heart-shaped sponges
▲ potatoes (cut in half)
▲ scissors
▲ purple ink pad
▲ construction paper

RAINBOW WHIRLPOOLS

MATERIALS

▲ pie tins

▲ whole milk (room temperature)

▲ red, blue, and yellow food coloring

▲ eyedroppers

▲ liquid dish-washing soap

Divide the class into small groups. Give each group a pie tin two-thirds full of whole milk. In each pie tin, place three drops of each color (red at 12 o'clock, blue at 4 o'clock, and yellow at 8 o'clock). Ask students to predict what will happen when a few drops of soap are added to the milk. Invite students to use eyedroppers to add a few drops of soap to the milk. Explain that the soap breaks the milk's surface tension (a force that causes the milk to behave as if a thin, elastic film covers the surface) and causes the colors to swirl and mix, creating secondary colors and a rainbow whirlpool.

FLYING RAINBOWS

MATERIALS

▲ 3 ½" (9 cm) paper squares (rainbow colors)

▲ glue

A rainbow may look like an arc, but it is really a full circle. The earth's horizon blocks half of it from our view. Give each student 8 different-colored paper squares to make flying rainbows. Have students fold one of their squares in half so the crease is at the top. Then, have them fold down the upper-left corner so it meets the center of the bottom. Have students fold up the lower-right corner, forming a parallelogram. Ask students to repeat the process with the other squares. To assemble the flier, help students fit the open triangle of one parallelogram into the triangular pocket of the next, working clockwise to complete a circle. Invite students to dab glue between the pieces to secure them. Take students outside to fly their rainbow rings.

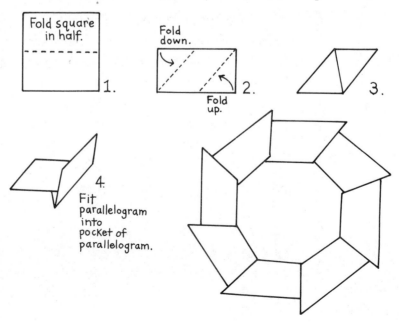

RAINBOW BOOKS

Discuss with students different objects that are usually certain colors, such as red tomatoes and cherries, orange basketballs and pumpkins, yellow sunflowers and bananas, green clovers and lettuce, blue skies and blueberries, and purple eggplants and violets. Have students draw objects in the same color on each of six sheets of drawing paper. Help students complete the sentence *I see (color) (objects)*. For example, *I see red fire trucks, roses, and stop signs.* Have students complete the sentence for each color of the rainbow. Bind the pages to make individual books using construction-paper covers. Invite each student to draw a rainbow on the cover and title it *My Rainbow-Colored World.*

RAINBOW OF FRIENDS

HOME ACTIVITY

Photocopy student photographs and shape the photocopies into ovals. Glue the ovals on a sheet of drawing paper in rainbow-like arcs and write on the paper *A Rainbow of Friends in Room _____.* Make photocopies (one per student) of the drawing, cut each photocopy into puzzle shapes, and place each set of shapes in a separate envelope. Decorate a canvas bag with rainbows and fill it with one of the envelopes, a set of water-colors or dot paints, a paper towel, a place mat, a cup, and a copy of *A Rainbow of My Own.* Send the bag home with a student. Have the student read the book with his or her family, put the puzzle together, glue it to another piece of paper, and paint the class photos with a rainbow of colors! The students may keep the rainbow puzzle, but must return the bag for the next student to take home.

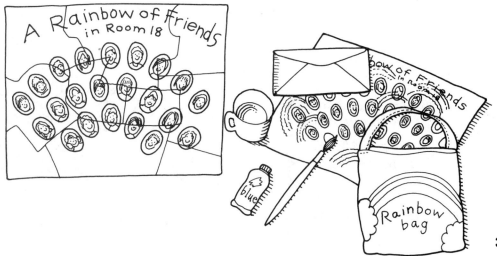

PIG DAY

March 1

Students will go hog wild celebrating National Pig Day. They will love to "ham it up." Share delightful pig tales with your students and have a pig-out picnic. Students won't find these activities "boar"ing.

LITERATURE LINKS

Book of Pigericks
by Arnold Lobel

Perfect the Pig
by Susan Jeschke

Pig Pig Grows Up
by David McPhail

Piggins by Jane Yolen

The Piggy in the Puddle
by Charlotte Pomerantz

Pigs by Robert Munsch

Pigs Aplenty, Pigs Galore!
by David McPhail

Pigs Will Be Pigs
by Amy Axelrod

Pigsty by Mark Teague

Yummers! by James Marshall

TEN LITTLE PIGGIES

Lay down brown butcher paper or a brown blanket as mud. Give each student one egg carton cup to make a pig snout. Have students paint cups pink and let dry. Invite students to paint black nostril holes and staple elastic to the sides. Invite groups of ten to act out the song "Ten Little Piggies" while wearing their pig snouts. Ask each "piggy" to jump in the "mud" one at a time. Sing the song again and stop between verses to have students create addition facts to match the piggies in the mud. Practice subtraction facts with students as the piggies get out of the mud.

MATERIALS
▲ brown butcher paper or brown blanket
▲ egg cartons
▲ scissors
▲ pink and black paint/paintbrushes
▲ stapler
▲ elastic

Ten Little Piggies
(to the tune of "Ten Little Indians")

One little, two little, three little piggies,
Four little, five little, six little piggies,
Seven little, eight little, nine little piggies,
Ten little muddy piggies!

Ten little, nine little, eight little piggies,
Seven little, six little, five little piggies,
Four little, three little, two little piggies,
One little muddy piggy!

HEY, PIGS!

Read aloud *Pigs.* In the story, pigs run out of their pen to some unusual places, including the principal's office. Discuss with students other places the pigs could visit. Invite students to write and illustrate these places. Copy the Pig reproducible on pink construction paper and have students cut out the parts. Have students glue the pig head and hooves to the top of their paper and the tail to the back of the paper so it hangs below.

MATERIALS
▲ *Pigs* by Robert Munsch
▲ writing paper
▲ Pig reproducible (page 38)
▲ pink construction paper
▲ scissors
▲ glue

PIGGY POETRY

Copy on sentence strips the poem "I Like Pigs!" from the reproducible (an adaptation of Margaret Wise Brown's "I Like Bugs"). As a class, brainstorm words that describe pigs and list them on sentence strips. Have students choose descriptive words to complete the first and third stanzas. Then, brainstorm and list prepositional phrases of places where pigs might be found. Invite students to choose four to complete the middle stanza. Chant the poem as a class several different ways by changing the descriptive words and phrases. Invite students to complete the reproducible with their favorite version.

PIG

I LIKE PIGS!

_____ pigs

_____ pigs

_____ pigs

Any kind of pigs.

I like pigs!

Pigs_____

Pigs_____

Pigs_____

Pigs_____

I like pigs!

_____ pigs

_____ pigs

_____ pigs

Any kind of pigs.

I like pigs!

DR. SEUSS'S BIRTHDAY

PAPER PLATE PAINTED RED

6"

CONSTRUCTION PAPER WITH PAINTED RED STRIPES

red

March 2

Dr. Seuss has charmed generations of readers with his clever rhymes, silly names, and fantastic creatures. Celebrate Dr. Seuss's birthday with these zany activities. Your students may discover (like Sam I Am) that they like green eggs and ham.

LITERATURE LINKS

Books by Dr. Seuss

The 500 Hats of Bartholomew Cubbins

And to Think That I Saw It on Mulberry Street

The Cat in the Hat

Green Eggs and Ham

Horton Hatches the Egg

I Can Read with My Eyes Shut

McElligot's Pool

My Many Colored Days

Sneetches and Other Stories

DR. SEUSS HATS

After reading *The Cat in the Hat*, invite students to make Dr. Seuss hats. Ask students to turn white construction paper lengthwise and paint red horizontal stripes. Then have them turn paper plates upside down and paint them red. When they dry, cut out a 6" (15 cm) circle from the center of each paper plate. Help students roll the striped paper into a cylinder and fit it into the paper-plate opening, staple the cylinder so it stays closed, and then staple the cylinder to the paper plate. Have students punch a hole on each side of their plates and tie black yarn to each side. Invite students to try on their hats and tie the yarn under their chins. Take pictures of students wearing their Dr. Seuss hats for the So Many Hats Book activity (page 41).

(page 41).

MATERIALS
- ▲ *The Cat in the Hat* by Dr. Seuss
- ▲ 12" x 18" (30.5 cm x 46 cm) white construction paper
- ▲ red paint/paintbrushes
- ▲ sturdy paper plates
- ▲ scissors
- ▲ stapler
- ▲ hole punch
- ▲ black yarn
- ▲ camera/film

SO MANY HATS BOOK

Cut photocopy paper in half and cut out a small circle in the center of each page so photographs of student faces show through the circles. Staple six pages together for each student book. Make templates of the Hat Book reproducible on tagboard. Have students fold construction paper in half and trace the hat templates on the folded paper so the top of the hat is on the fold. Have each student cut out the hat shape, being careful not to cut along the fold. Staple the six pages inside the hat book covers. Help students glue to the last page photos of themselves wearing their Dr. Seuss hats, positioned so that their faces show through the holes. Have students copy on the first page the sentence *There are so many hats that you will see. Which one do you like best on me?* Have students copy on pages 2–5 the sentence *I wear a _____ hat to _____.* Ask students to draw a different hat on each page (for pages 2–5) above the photo and complete the sentences to correspond with the illustrations. On the last page, have students write *For fun, I wear my Dr. Seuss hat. What do you think of that?* Invite students to read their books to family members at home.

GREEN EGGS AND HAM

Read aloud *Green Eggs and Ham.* Give each student a copy of the Green Eggs and Ham recipe. Ask students to read the directions as you make the meal. Serve students and, after they have tasted the meal, ask them to draw a face on the recipe showing how much (or little!) they liked it. Make a bar graph on chart paper titled *Do You Like Green Eggs and Ham?* Have students draw happy faces if they liked it and sad faces if they did not on construction-paper squares and attach the squares to the graph.

MATERIALS

▲ *The Cat in the Hat* by Dr. Seuss
▲ Hat pattern (page 45)
▲ red and white construction paper
▲ scissors
▲ glue
▲ markers or paint/paint-brushes
▲ masking tape

WHAT'S IN THAT HAT?

After reading *The Cat in the Hat*, invite students to choose different animals to be in a hat. Ask students to create rhyming activities the animal did. For example, *The fish in the hat made a wish* or *The spider in the hat drank cider*. Have students complete the frame *The _____ in the hat _____*. Enlarge the hat pattern and trace it on red construction paper. Invite students to cut out the hats. Have students cut white construction-paper stripes and glue them on the hat. Have students each draw and cut out a large picture of the animal they chose, slide the bottom through the hat opening, and tape the picture so the animal looks like it is popping out of the hat.

The bee in the hat stung me!

MATERIALS

▲ *My Many Colored Days* by Dr. Seuss
▲ scissors
▲ paint/paintbrushes
▲ construction paper
▲ sponges
▲ bookbinding materials

OUR MANY COLORED DAYS

Read aloud *My Many Colored Days*, and discuss how different colors can evoke different emotions. Have students cut gingerbread-people shapes from white construction paper similar to the ones in the story. Ask students to paint the shapes one color and let dry. Invite each student to add eyes, a nose, and a smile. Have students sponge-paint a white construction-paper background and when dry, glue the shapes to it. Ask students how the color makes them feel. Encourage them to try to rhyme using the frame *When my days are (describing word) and (color), I _____*. For example, *When my days are sad and blue, I sometimes sit with nothing to do*. Have students write their rhymes below their pictures. Combine pages into a class book titled *Our Many Colored Days in Room _____*.

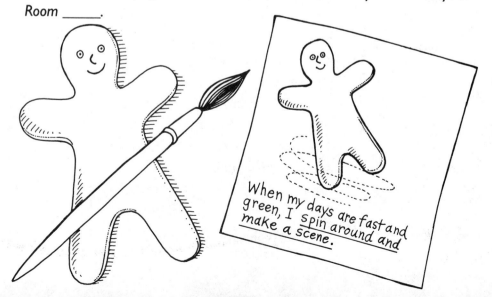

When my days are fast and green, I spin around and make a scene.

HAT BOOK

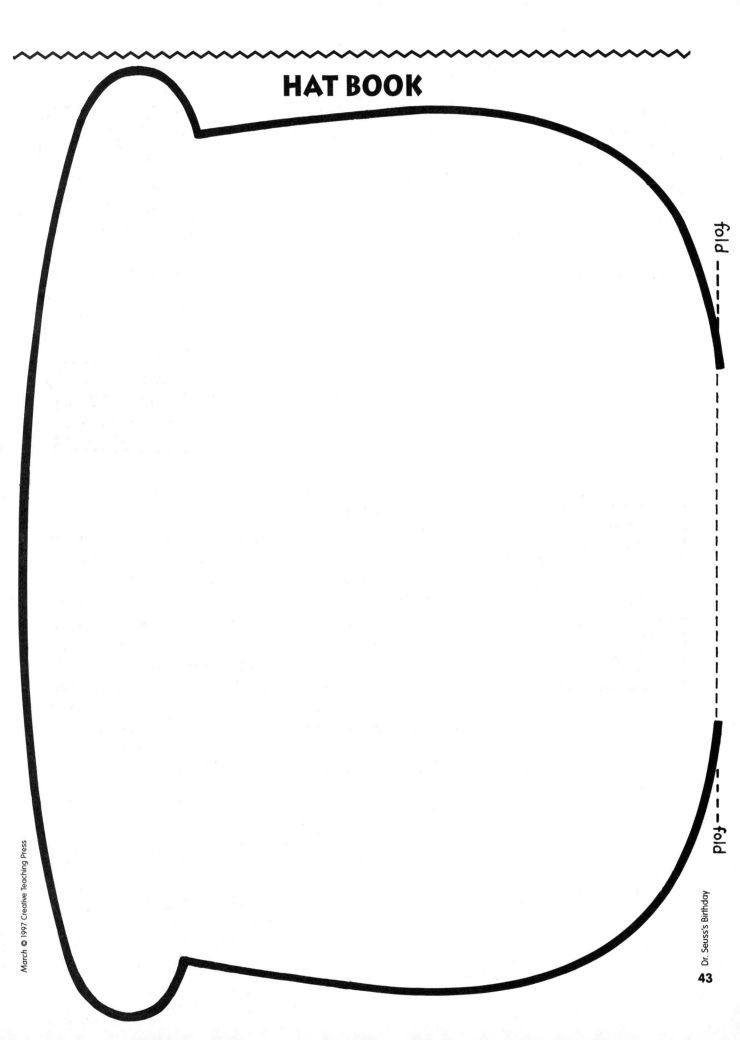

fold

fold

Dr. Seuss's Birthday

43

GREEN EGGS AND HAM

By Chef _____

1. Melt butter in skillet and crack eggs.

2. Add green food coloring and mix.

3. Add sliced ham and scramble.

4. Do you like green eggs and ham?

Dr. Seuss's Birthday

44

March © 1997 Creative Teaching Press

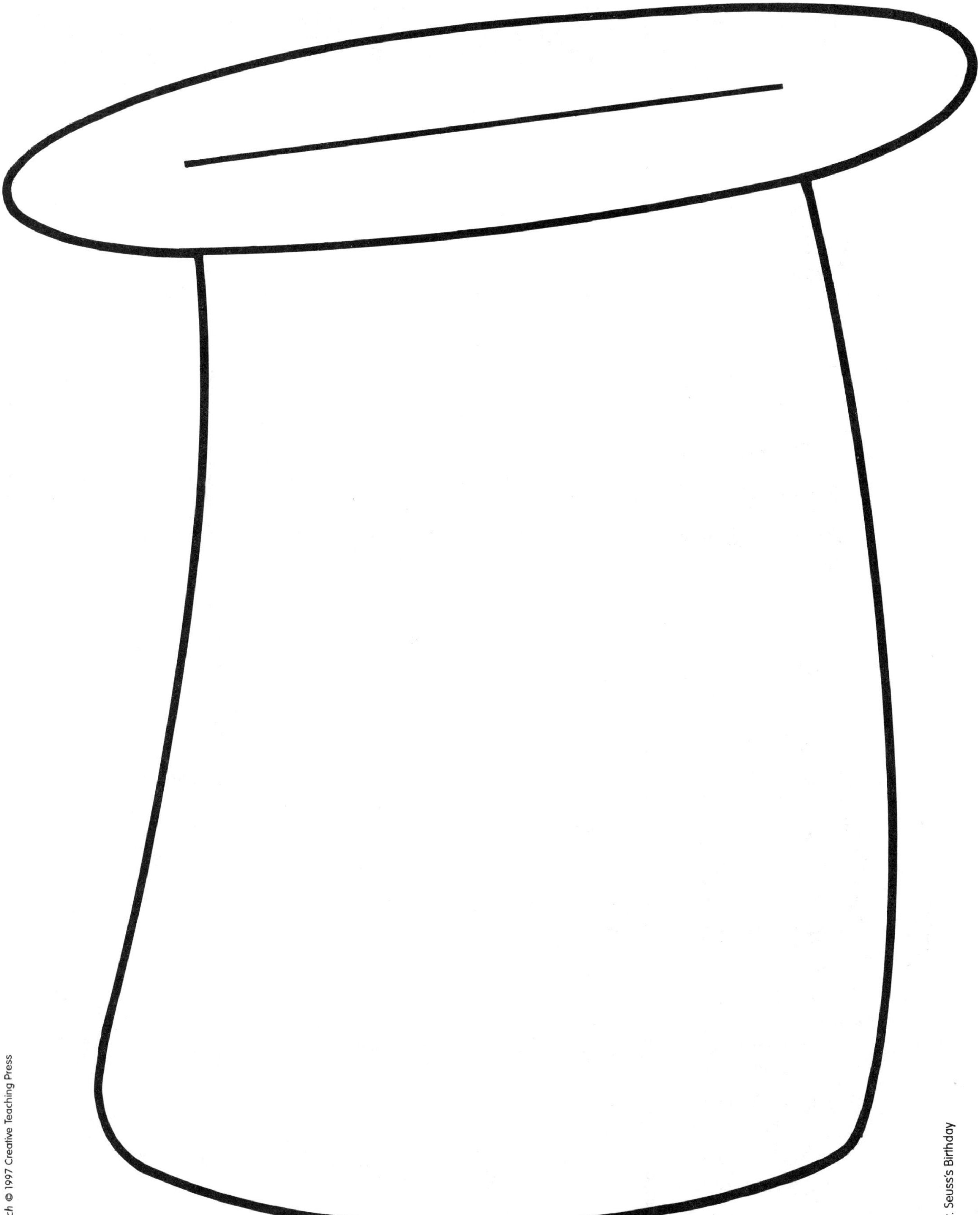

DAISY DAY

Luther Burbank's birthday is March 7. Burbank created the Shasta daisy, the spineless cactus, the Burbank potato, and the nectarine. Watch your students blossom with these flowering activities.

LITERATURE LINKS

Barney Bipple's Magic Dandelions by Carol Chapman

Chrysanthemum by Kevin Henkes

Daisy-Head Mayzie by Dr. Seuss

Flower Garden by Eve Bunting

Frog and Toad Together by Arnold Lobel

Linnea's Windowsill Garden by Christina Bjork and Lena Anderson

The Reason for a Flower by Ruth Heller

A Seed Is a Promise by Claire Merrill

The Tiny Seed by Eric Carle

SHASTA DAISY HAT

Read aloud *Daisy-Head Mayzie.* After story discussion, have each student fold a yellow construction-paper strip in half lengthwise. Help students hole-punch each end of the strip. Have students poke brass fasteners through the holes and hook a rubber band around the fasteners. Invite students to cut daisy petals from white construction paper and glue them to the yellow construction-paper headband. Invite students to sing the "Five Little Flowers" chant in groups of five while wearing their daisy hats.

MATERIALS
- ▲ *Daisy-Head Mayzie* by Dr. Seuss
- ▲ 6" x 18" (15 cm x 46 cm) yellow construction-paper strips
- ▲ hole punch
- ▲ brass fasteners
- ▲ large rubber bands
- ▲ white construction paper
- ▲ scissors

Five Little Flowers
(to the tune of "Itsy Bitsy Spider")

Five little flowers, Looking for the sun.	*Students look up.*
See their heads nodding, Bowing one by one.	*Students nod their heads and bow.*
Down, down, down, Falls the gentle rain.	*Students wiggle their fingers and shrink to the ground.*
And the five little flowers Pop up their heads again.	*Students pop up.*

Motions

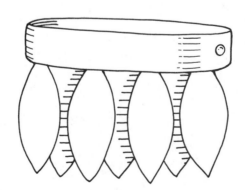

DAISY DIALOGUE

Tell students that Luther Burbank talked to his plants to help them grow and some people play music for, sing to, or gently touch their plants' leaves to help their plants grow. Read aloud "The Garden" from *Frog and Toad Together*. Ask students what they think helped the seeds grow. Brainstorm, and list on chart paper, different things to do to help seeds grow. Give each student a few daisy seeds. Invite each student to poke a small hole in the bottom of two Styrofoam cups, fill them with potting soil, and place the seeds on top. Have students water their seeds so the soil is moist. Remind students that plants need sunlight and water to grow. Invite students to take their seeds home. Have students talk to and play music for only one of the seed cups. Have students report back to school which plant germinates first and which looks healthier.

MATERIALS
- ▲ *Frog and Toad Together* by Arnold Lobel
- ▲ chart paper
- ▲ Styrofoam cups
- ▲ potting soil
- ▲ daisy seeds

How Does Your Garden Grow?

Sing to your seeds.
Read them stories.
Visit your seeds each day.
Water your seeds.
Play the piano for them.
Give them compliments.

DARLING DAISIES

MATERIALS
- ▲ construction paper
- ▲ scissors
- ▲ paint/paintbrushes
- ▲ tongue depressors
- ▲ colored tissue paper
- ▲ glue
- ▲ sandpaper
- ▲ yogurt cups
- ▲ hair spray
- ▲ tagboard

Have students draw and cut out construction-paper daisy shapes and leaves. Invite students to paint tongue depressor "stems" and let them dry. Have students tear up small pieces of colored tissue paper, scrunch them into balls, and glue them to the center of the daisies. Students can glue "daisies" and "leaves" to their "stems." Invite students to rub yogurt cups with sandpaper and spray them with hair spray to help the paint stick to the cups. Invite students to paint the containers and let them dry. Have students turn the cups upside down on tagboard, trace around them, and cut out the circles. Students can paint the circles to resemble soil. Help students poke a hole in the center of the soil circles for the flower stem to go through. Ask students to push the stems through the holes and glue the "soil" circles to the tops of the yogurt containers to hold the flowers in place.

HAMBURGER AND PICKLE DAY

Beef up your March curriculum during National Hamburger and Pickle Month with these juicy activities!

THE GREAT BIG ENORMOUS HAMBURGER

After reading *The Great, Enormous Hamburger*, discuss students' favorite hamburger ingredients. Have students each create a favorite hamburger ingredient from construction paper and sort themselves according to their favorite items. Have students start with the bottom buns and build one enormous hamburger, stacking and gluing their items on butcher paper in the order given in the "My Yummy Hamburger" poem (page 50). When they have finished, ask students what observations they can make about their enormous hamburger, such as what were the most and least popular ingredients and how many more students chose one ingredient than chose another. Record comments on sentence strips placed around the hamburger.

MATERIALS

▲ *The Great, Enormous Hamburger* by Jillian Cutting
▲ construction paper (light and dark brown, light and dark green, red, orange, yellow)
▲ scissors
▲ glue
▲ butcher paper
▲ Hamburger and Pickle reproducible (page 50)
▲ sentence strips

HAMBURGERS IN A BOX

HAMBURGERS IN A BOX

MATERIALS

▲ 6" (15 cm) construction-paper squares (light and dark brown, yellow, red, light and dark green)
▲ index cards
▲ hamburger boxes (available from most fast-food chains)
▲ library-card pockets

Decide on a number combination to work on, such as combinations of six (0+6, 5+1, 4+2, 3+3). Invite students to cut several hamburger ingredients from construction paper, including light-brown buns, yellow hole-punched cheese, dark-brown meat, red tomatoes, light-green lettuce, and long dark-green pickles. Have each student write the combinations on index cards, place them in a library-card pocket, and tape the pocket to the inside of a hamburger box. Students can label the lid _____'s *Burger Combinations*. Have students pull out one card at a time and use the burger pieces to illustrate their combinations. For example, 4+2 could equal 4 pickles and 2 slices of cheese, or 1+5 could equal one meat patty and five tomatoes. Have students return burger pieces to their boxes and take them home to practice with family members.

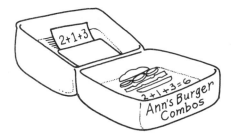

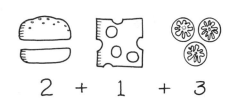

2 + 1 + 3

TEENY TINY BURGERS

MATERIALS

▲ *The Great, Enormous Hamburger* by Jillian Cutting
▲ small sausage patties
▲ electric skillet
▲ small dinner rolls
▲ American cheese slices (cut in fourths)
▲ condiments (pickles, ketchup, mustard)
▲ paper plates
▲ napkins
▲ drawing paper
▲ bookbinding materials

After reading *The Great, Enormous Hamburger*, invite your students to make teeny tiny burgers. Cook small sausages in an electric frying skillet. Invite students to add condiments to their "burgers." Have students each draw a picture of their burgers and complete below the drawing the sentence *My Teeny Tiny Burger had _____*. Place stories in a *Teeny Tiny Burger Book.*

My Teeny Tiny Burger had teeny tiny cheese and a pickle.

HAMBURGER AND PICKLE PLACE MATS

MATERIALS

▲ scissors
▲ construction paper
▲ glue
▲ Hamburger and Pickle reproducible (page 50)
▲ crayons or markers

Have each student cut hamburger parts from construction paper and glue them on large construction paper in sequence, according to the poem. Have students cut out the poem and glue it above their burgers. Invite students to draw on their place mats next to the pickle poem interesting foods to eat with pickles.

HAMBURGER AND PICKLE

My Yummy Hamburger

First we need a bottom bun,
Then we add the meat.
Next come cheese and pickles,
Mustard, ketchup, oh, so sweet.
Add lettuce and tomato,
The top bun goes on last.
My hamburger is ready.
Yum, Yum! Let's eat it fast!

Pickles

I put pickles on popcorn, pickles on pancakes,
Pickles in pumpkin pie.
I put pickles on pizza, pickles in pasta.
You'll like it if you try!

March © 1997 Creative Teaching Press

TELEPHONE DAY

March 10

On this date in 1876, Alexander Graham Bell transmitted the first telephone message to his assistant, saying, "Mr. Watson, come here, I want you!" Celebrate Telephone Day by teaching students proper phone etiquette and how to make their own phone.

LITERATURE LINKS

101 Telephone Jokes
by Katy Hall

Case of the Missing Dumb Bells
by Crosby Newell Bousall

Phone Book (Pop-Up)
by Jan Pienkowski
and Ann Carter

Soup Should Be Seen, Not Heard!
by Beth Brainard and Sue Behr

Telephones (Inventors and Inventions)
by Gini Holland and Amy Stone

TELEPHONE TALK

Read aloud the chapter on telephone etiquette from *Soup Should Be Seen, Not Heard!* After story discussion, practice telephone etiquette with students. Have the students role-play situations, such as calling a parent at work, dialing emergency numbers, and answering the phone when parents aren't home. Have students practice saying *They can't come to the phone right now, may I take a message?* Have students practice writing down a phone number given over the phone. Discuss with the class information that should be recorded when a telephone message is taken, such as who is calling, the phone number, the date and time, and a short message. Have students write their phone numbers on the Phone reproducible, cut out the phone, and tie string to the holes. Invite students to work with partners to practice using their own phones. Explain when students need to dial number 1 and the area code.

MATERIALS
▲ *Soup Should Be Seen, Not Heard!* by Beth Brainard and Sue Behr
▲ toy or real telephones
▲ Phone reproducible (page 53)
▲ scissors
▲ string

My home telephone number:
805 - 555 - 9292

EMERGENCY 911

Remind students that 911 is the number they should call in an emergency. Describe to students different situations that require dialing 911, such as *Your baby-sitter fell down and cannot get up* or *A family member is choking.* Describe situations that do not require dialing 911, such as *You are at your friend's house, the power goes out, and you want to make sure everything's all right; You want to know what time it is so you won't get home too late; You want to see if the 911 number really works; You have a question for a police officer; A car has been parked in front of your house for a week.* Have students put their thumbs up if they think a situation requires them to call 911. Have them put their thumbs down if it's not an emergency. Explain it is important not to misuse 911 because someone with a real emergency might need to get through. Describe situations in which calling 911 is appropriate. Have students take the Emergency Phone Numbers Booklet home.

NUMBER, PLEASE!

Have students construct telephone models. Divide the class into pairs. Help students use a toothpick to poke a hole in the bottom of a plastic cup. Have one student from each pair thread one end of string through the bottom of a cup and tie it to the center of a toothpick to hold the string in place. Have their partners do the same with the other end of the string. Have the partners each hold a cup and stand far enough apart from each other so the string between the cups is taut. Have one student talk through the telephone while the other puts the cup next to his or her ear to listen. Encourage students to try talking softly and then louder to see what happens.

PHONE

My home telephone number:

(___ ___) ___ ___ ___ - ___ ___ ___ ___

EMERGENCY PHONE NUMBERS BOOKLET

Dear Family,
I'm learning how to use the telephone during emergencies. After I cut apart the pages and staple them together, will you please help me complete the Emergency Phone Numbers Booklet so I will remember who to call in case of an emergency? Let's keep the booklet near the telephone!

My Emergency Phone Numbers	In case of emergency, I will say	Police, Fire, Medical
Name _____ _____	My address is _____ _____ I need help because _____ _____	911
Parents at Work _____ _____	Friend, Neighbor, or Relative _____ _____	Poison Control _____ _____

Telephone Day

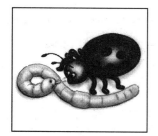

CREEPY CRITTER DAY

March is an ideal time to explore the great outdoors and examine bugs. Kids love creepy critters, so invite them to share their favorite bugs and "dig in" to these creepy, crawly activities.

LITERATURE LINKS

101 Wacky Facts about Bugs and Spiders
by Jean Waricha

Amazing Insects
by Laurence Mound

Backyard Bugs
by Robin K. Laughlin

The Best Bug Parade
by Stuart J. Murphy

Bugs!
by Patricia and Fredrick McKissack

The Bugs Go Marching
CTP Learn to Read Series

Build Your Own Bugs
by Dennis Schatz

How Many Bugs in a Box?
by David A. Carter

The Icky Bug Counting Book
by Jerry Pallotta

BUGS IN A BOX

Read aloud *How Many Bugs in a Box?* Invite students to work in small groups to decorate crayon boxes and create unique bugs from art supplies. Ask students to put their bugs in their boxes. Have each group use descriptive words to complete on a paper strip the sentence *How many bugs in a/an _____ box?* and glue it to the outside of the box. Have each group write a descriptive answer and glue it to the inside lid. Invite groups to display their boxes on a table so others can peek inside and count the bugs in each box.

MATERIALS

▲ *How Many Bugs in a Box?* by David A. Carter

▲ empty crayon boxes (64 count, if possible)

▲ art supplies (paint, paintbrushes, markers, crayons, pipe cleaners, construction-paper scraps, wiggly eyes, pom-poms, etc.)

CAMOUFLAGED CRITTERS

MATERIALS

▲ small, colored objects (toothpicks, construction-paper squares, buttons)
▲ construction paper
▲ stapler
▲ elastic
▲ paper cups
▲ chart paper
▲ markers
▲ pictures of camouflaged insects

Place in a grassy area small, colored objects to represent bugs. Have students make bird-beak masks by rolling construction paper into funnels, stapling them closed, and attaching elastic. Take the class to the grassy area, and divide it into two teams. Line teams up single file and have a relay race in which students "fly" into the grassy area, place the first "bug" they see in a paper cup, and fly back "home." When the relay is finished, return to class to compare captured bugs.

Have the first "bird" from each team share his or her bug first, followed in order by the other birds. (The first birds will most likely have brightly colored bugs.) Use markers of different colors to list on chart paper the colors of the bugs. Ask students to make observations on the order and frequency of the captured bugs. Share pictures of camouflaged insects and discuss how color patterns help bugs hide from their enemies.

DIRT AND WORM NESTS

MATERIALS

▲ instant chocolate pudding mix
▲ chocolate sandwich cookies
▲ blender
▲ green plastic cups
▲ gummy worm candy
▲ plastic spoons

Mix pudding according to package directions. Crumble cookies in a blender and mix them with the pudding. Layer the mixture with gummy worms in individual green "flowerpot" cups and serve to students. Invite students to dig into the "nest" with spoons to find chewy gummy worms.

1. Make chocolate pudding.

2. Crumble cookies in a blender and mix with pudding.

3. Open a bag of gummy worms.

4. Layer the cup with pudding mixture and gummy worms.

5. Dig in!

PAJAMA DAY

Wake up those sleepyheads with a pajama party. Have everyone wear pajamas to school and make donuts and hot cocoa with your students for an unforgettable day.

LITERATURE LINKS

Arthur's First Sleepover
by Marc Brown

Bearsie Bear and the Surprise Sleepover Party
by Bernard Waber

Best Friends Sleep Over
by Jacqueline Rogers

Daisy Rabbit's Tree House
by Penny Dale

Edward's Overwhelming Overnight
by Rosemary Wells

Franklin Has a Sleepover
by Paulette Bourgeois

I Can't Sleep
CTP Learn to Read Series

Ira Sleeps Over
by Bernard Waber

Pajama Party by Amy Hest

Porcupine's Pajama Party
by Doug Cushman and
Terry Webb Harshman

PAJAMA PARTY

Invite students to bring pillows and wear their pajamas and slippers to school. Give each student a serving of dough and invite students to make a hole in the center. Ask a parent volunteer to deep-fry each donut in oil. Invite students to place their cooked donut in a paper lunch sack, pour a spoonful of a donut topping inside, and shake. Serve hot cocoa. Turn out the lights and read a bedtime story using a flashlight. Have students write about their pajama party on the Pillow reproducible and bind their stories into a class book.

MATERIALS
▲ Pop-n-Fresh® dough
▲ oil
▲ electric wok
▲ donut toppings (cinnamon sugar, powdered sugar, brown sugar, sprinkles)
▲ paper lunch sacks
▲ napkins
▲ cups
▲ instant hot cocoa
▲ electric tea kettle
▲ bedtime story
▲ flashlight
▲ Pillow reproducible (page 59)
▲ bookbinding materials

MATERIALS

▲ *Ira Sleeps Over* by Bernard Waber

▲ 3" (7.5 cm) construction-paper squares

▲ sentence strips

I SLEEP WITH . . .

Read aloud *Ira Sleeps Over.* After story discussion, invite students to bring to class something they love to sleep with, such as a stuffed animal, doll, or blanket. Invite students to share their special objects. Students can draw pictures of their items on construction-paper squares and attach them to a bar graph. Write student observations on sentence strips around the graph. Invite students to work together to sort their items into different categories. Afterward, invite a few students to act out *Ira Sleeps Over.*

MATERIALS

▲ *Best Friends Sleep Over* by Jacqueline Rogers

▲ construction paper

▲ paint/paintbrushes

▲ scissors

▲ butcher-paper vines

IT'S A JUNGLE OUT THERE

Read aloud *Best Friends Sleep Over.* Invite students to paint jungle animals wearing pajamas. Have students cut out their animals and give them alliterative names such as Monkey Mark or Gabi Gorilla. Hang the animals from construction-paper vines on a bulletin board titled *(Teacher's name)'s Pajama Party.* Ask students to dictate sentences about their animals. Record them on sentence strips around the bulletin board.

SAVE-A-SPIDER DAY

Don't stomp or smash a spider or wipe out its web—not on March 14. It's Save-a-Spider Day! Students will love making spider webs and chocolate spiders!

LITERATURE LINKS

Anansi and the Moss-Covered Rock retold by Eric A. Kimmel

Anansi the Spider by Gerald McDermott

Be Nice to Spiders by Margaret B. Graham

The Itsy Bitsy Spider by Iza Trapani

Miss Spider's Tea Party by David Kirk

The Roly Poly Spider by Jill Sardegna

Spiders, Spiders Everywhere! CTP Learn to Read Series

The Very Busy Spider by Eric Carle

ITSY BITSY SPIDER NECKLACES

Have students fold the Itsy Bitsy Spider reproducible in half and cut along the dotted line halfway through the paper. Have students hold the paper with the cut at top and fold the left flap forward and the right flap backward. Ask students to keep the flaps folded while they open the paper, and have them fold the paper in half so the pictures face out. Have students fold the paper again, making sure page one is in front. Help students hole-punch the top of their books. Have students decorate their book with markers and add blue sequin raindrops and a small plastic spider on the waterspout. Invite students to thread ribbon or yarn through the holes and wear their itsy bitsy spider necklaces.

MATERIALS
- ▲ Itsy Bitsy Spider reproducible (page 62)
- ▲ scissors
- ▲ hole punch
- ▲ markers
- ▲ blue sequins
- ▲ small plastic spiders
- ▲ ribbon or yarn

SPIDERS, SPIDERS IN A WEB

MATERIALS

▲ 1 cup (250 ml) white flour
▲ 1 cup (250 ml) salt
▲ 1 cup (250 ml) water
▲ large bowl
▲ mixing spoon
▲ plastic squeeze bottles
▲ blue construction paper
▲ black tempera paint
▲ glue
▲ wiggly eyes

Mix the flour, salt, and water in a bowl and pour into plastic squeeze bottles. Show students how to draw a large spider web. Have students use the squeeze bottles to make their own spider webs on blue construction paper. When the webs dry, have students paint their hands black and place their wrists together, left hands facing left and right hands facing right, so their thumbs form spider mandibles, or teeth. Have students press their hands in the center of their web to form a spider. When the handprints dry, have students glue wiggly eyes on their "spiders." Ask students to name their spiders, paint an insect caught in the web, and write _____ caught a _____ in its web.

Delphine caught a fly in its web.

SPIDER HEADBANDS

MATERIALS

▲ 6" x 18" (15 cm x 46 cm) black construction paper
▲ 1" x 9" (2.5 cm x 23 cm) black construction-paper strips
▲ hole-reinforcement rings
▲ stapler
▲ hole punch
▲ brass fasteners
▲ rubber bands

Have students fold black construction paper in half lengthwise to form a headband. Ask each student to accordion-fold eight black construction-paper strips for spider legs and staple four on each side of the headband. Invite each student to add two hole-reinforcement rings for eyes. Help each student hole-punch each end of the headband, put in brass fasteners, and hook a rubber band around the fasteners.

CHOCOLATE SPIDERS

MATERIALS

▲ electric skillet
▲ chocolate chips
▲ Chinese noodles
▲ waxed paper
▲ M&Ms

Melt chocolate chips. Have each student arrange eight Chinese noodles on a piece of waxed paper to be spider legs. Drop a spoonful of chocolate in the middle of each set of legs and invite students to rearrange the legs and add M&M eyes. As a class, count the "spider" legs by eights and brainstorm other things that have eight parts (octagon sides and an octopus's legs).

Chill the spiders 30 minutes and then enjoy!

5

Out came the sun

6

and dried up all the rain.

4

and washed the spider out.

7

So the itsy bitsy spider

3

Down came the rain

8

went up the spout again.

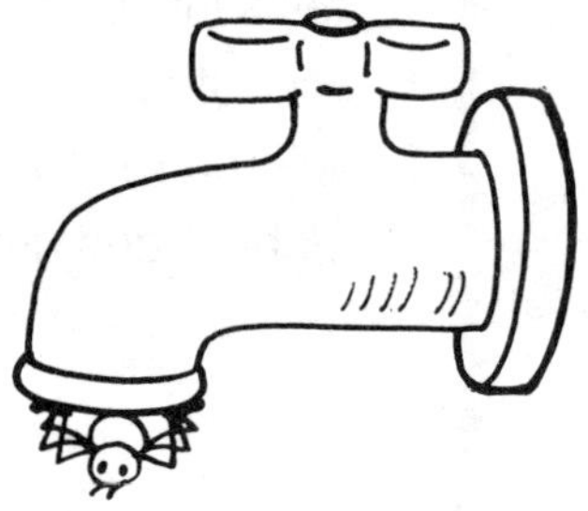

2

went up the waterspout.

1

The itsy bitsy spider

ST. PATRICK'S DAY

March 17

Wear green or you may get pinched on St. Patrick's Day! March 17, A.D. 389 is the birthday of St. Patrick of Scotland. According to legend, St. Patrick charmed the snakes of Ireland into the sea and used the shamrock as a symbol of the Trinity when he preached. Tell students to be on the lookout for leprechauns, rainbows, and four-leaf clovers.

LITERATURE LINKS

Clever Tom and the Leprechaun
by Linda Shute

Hungry Leprechaun
by Mary Calhoun

Jamie O'Rourke and the Big Potato
by Tomie dePaola

St. Patrick's Day
by Gail Gibbons

LOCATE THE LEPRECHAUNS

Stage a visit from a leprechaun. A week before St. Patrick's Day, prepare tiny items for students to find each morning, such as gold coins, green doll furniture and shoes, green sponge-painted footprints, and gold spray-painted rocks. Mess up the room by turning over a few chairs. When students arrive, ask them if they can help you find clues to determine what happened. When they find a few clues, warn them to watch for leprechauns. Have students make "Wanted" posters for the mischievous leprechaun who messes up their room each day. Hang up the posters around the classroom and in school hallways or the cafeteria. Invite students to make the Shamrock Spectacles (page 64) to help them search for leprechauns. Have students write letters to the leprechaun on writing paper. Ask students to cut only on the dotted lines of the Leprechaun reproducible. Have students staple their writing paper to the bottom portion and fold the reproducible on the fold line so the bottom portion tucks under the leprechaun's chin. Tell students you will leave their letters for the leprechaun. Ask an upper-grade teacher to have his or her students respond to the letters, pretending to be the leprechaun.

MATERIALS
- ▲ chocolate gold coins
- ▲ doll furniture and shoes
- ▲ green paint
- ▲ tiny shoe-shaped sponges
- ▲ gold spray-painted rocks
- ▲ Shamrock Spectacles reproducible (page 69)
- ▲ Leprechaun reproducible (page 68)
- ▲ 3" x 7" (7.5 cm x 18 cm) writing paper
- ▲ scissors
- ▲ stapler

WANTED:
Leprechaun
Left behind green shoes and gold coins.
REWARD!

SHAMROCK SPECTACLES

MATERIALS
- ▲ green construction paper
- ▲ Shamrock Spectacles reproducible (page 69)
- ▲ scissors
- ▲ green cellophane or plastic-wrap circles
- ▲ tape

Invite students to make shamrock spectacles to help them find leprechauns. Have students place the Shamrock Spectacles pattern on folded green construction paper and cut out the pattern. Help students cut out the eyeholes. Have students tape green cellophane or plastic-wrap circles across the eyeholes. Invite students to look through the shamrock spectacles in their search for leprechauns.

LEPRECHAUN TRAPS

MATERIALS
- ▲ shoe boxes
- ▲ art supplies (green tissue paper, tempera paint/paintbrushes, markers, green fabric scraps)
- ▲ drinking straws
- ▲ green yarn
- ▲ colored marshmallows
- ▲ chocolate gold coins
- ▲ green pen

Invite students to use art supplies to decorate shoe boxes to be Leprechaun traps. On St. Patrick's Day, have students get their traps ready to catch leprechauns! Instruct students to tie a piece of green yarn to a drinking straw and set their box upside down with the straw supporting the box. Have students sprinkle under the box a few marshmallows to serve as leprechaun bait. After students leave for the day, remove the marshmallows and replace them with chocolate gold coins and pull all the traps closed. Use a green pen to write a note to students informing them that the traps were good, but not quick enough and sign it *Lucky Leprechaun.* The next day, tell students that no one caught the leprechaun, but he did leave a note and some treats.

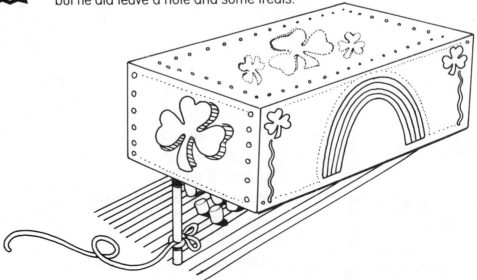

LIVELY LEPRECHAUNS

MATERIALS

▲ scissors

▲ green, orange, and yellow construction paper

▲ Leprechaun Costume reproducible (page 70)

▲ sentence strips

▲ glue

▲ stapler

Have students use the Leprechaun Costume reproducible as a pattern for cutting out yellow hats, orange beards, and green shamrocks from construction paper. Have students glue the hat and beard to a sentence strip so the hat extends above the strip and the beard extends below it. Invite students to glue the shamrocks to their hats. Staple strips together to fit students' heads. Invite students to sing "Little Leprechaun" while wearing their hats.

Little Leprechaun

(to the tune of "I'm a Little Teapot")

I'm a little leprechaun, short and fat.
Here is my shamrock; here is my hat.
People try to steal my gold from me.
But no one has as you can see!
I can hide behind the bushes and trees,
Or the rocks so no one sees.
If you want to get me, just try and see.
You'll soon agree, you can't catch me!

DO YOU BELIEVE IN LEPRECHAUNS?

MATERIALS

▲ 3" (7.5 cm) construction-paper squares

▲ crayons or markers

▲ pot-of-gold-shaped butcher paper

Ask students if they believe in leprechauns. Have students draw leprechaun faces on construction-paper squares and attach them to the yes or no column on a pot-of-gold-shaped graph. Invite students to speak in front of the class and attempt to persuade others to believe or not believe in leprechauns.

OUR FAVORITE POTATOES

MATERIALS
▲ potato-shaped brown construction paper
▲ crayons or markers

Potatoes are the main source of food in Ireland. Discuss different foods made from potatoes, such as hash browns, French fries, mashed potatoes, baked potatoes, and boiled potatoes. Ask students what they like to eat with their favorite potatoes. Have students copy and complete on potato-shaped brown construction paper the frame *I like to eat _____ with my potatoes.* Invite students to illustrate their favorite potatoes with their favorite toppings, such as French fries with mustard or mashed potatoes with gravy.

LEAPIN' LEPRECHAUNS

MATERIALS
▲ crayons or markers
▲ Leapin' Leprechaun reproducible (page 71)
▲ scissors
▲ brass fasteners
▲ string
▲ rulers

Have students color the leprechaun parts on the Leapin' Leprechaun reproducible. Invite students to cut out the parts and use brass fasteners to connect them. Have students tape string to the arms and legs and tie the strings to a ruler. Invite students to sing "The Leprechaun March" while maneuvering their leapin' leprechauns.

The Leprechaun March
(to the tune of "Twinkle, Twinkle, Little Star")

Leprechauns are marching by.
See how cute they wink their eye.
See them marching two by two.
Can't you see them wave to you?
I know St. Patrick's Day is near,
Because the leprechauns are here!

MATH MAGIC

Write *3-17 is St. Patrick's Day* on a piece of paper without letting anyone see it, and put the paper in a sealed envelope. Ask a volunteer to complete the following:

1. Write a three-digit number with three different digits not including zero or one.
2. Reverse the digits.
3. Subtract the smaller three-digit number from the larger.
4. Reverse the digits.
5. Add the two new numbers from steps 3 and 4.
6. Subtract 772.

The answer will always be 317!

Invite the volunteer to open the envelope and reveal the number.

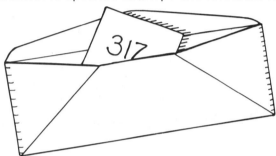

THE O'TEACHER'S FAMILY ALBUM

Decorate a canvas bag with green shamrocks. Title a blank journal *O'(Your name)'s St. Patrick's Day Family Album.* On the first page, draw a picture of your family wearing St. Patrick's Day hats and write *The O'(your name) Family.* Send home in the canvas bag the journal and markers, and have students draw under the caption *The O'(their name) Family,* a picture of their families wearing Irish hats.

LEPRECHAUN

fold up

SHAMROCK SPECTACLES

Five Little Leprechauns

Five little leprechauns,
Standing in a row.
One fell down
And hurt his toe.

Four little leprechauns,
Climbing in a tree.
One slipped down
While spying on me!

Three little leprechauns,
Dancing in the sun.
One sat down
And spoiled all the fun.

Two little leprechauns
Singing an Irish song.
One quit singing,
Said they sang too long.

One little leprechaun,
Guarding all the gold.
He fell asleep,
So I was told.

I crept to his cave,
As he began to snore.
I snatched up the gold
And ran out the door!

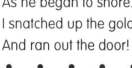

Place on fold.

St. Patrick's Day

LEPRECHAUN COSTUME

green hat

Fold line

orange beard

Fold line

yellow shamrock

March © 1997 Creative Teaching Press

LEAPIN' LEPRECHAUN

St. Patrick's Day

LUCKY DAY

Some people believe that a rabbit's foot or four-leaf clover can bring good luck. Whether or not you believe in luck, Lucky Day is meant to bring smiles, success, and the "luck o' the Irish" to an ordinary day.

LITERATURE LINKS

Angelita's Magic Yarn
by Doris Lecher

Did I Ever Tell You How Lucky You Are?
by Dr. Seuss

Fortunately by Remy Charlip

A Happy Tale
by Dorothy Butler

The Luckiest Kid on the Planet
by Lisa Campbell Ernst

The Luckiest One of All
by Bill Peet

A Piece of Luck
by Simon Henwood

Three Gold Pieces: A Greek Folk Tale
by Aliki

Wheel on the Chimney
by Margaret Wise Brown

HORSESHOES

In advance, cut out a cardboard horseshoe for each student. Invite students to color their horseshoes with markers to personalize them. Explain that some people hang a horseshoe above a door for good luck. Have students gather in groups of four. Go outdoors and place stakes in the ground for every group of four. Have students line up about 6' (2 m) from their group's stake. Invite two students from each group to take turns throwing their horseshoes toward their stake. The other two students in each group will be scorekeepers. After horseshoes are thrown, have scorekeepers tally the points. A ringer (horseshoe rings around the stake) is worth three points. A leaner (horseshoe leans on the stake) is worth two points. An almost (horseshoe is one horseshoe width away from the stake) is worth one point. Have scorekeepers trade places with players. Invite the groups to play three games and tally their scores.

MATERIALS
▲ scissors
▲ cardboard
▲ markers
▲ stakes

FIND A PENNY

Have students cut out the T-shirt and pocket from the Pocket reproducible. Then have them glue the pocket on three sides so the top remains open. Give each student a penny and discuss why it is lucky to find one. Invite students to drop the pennies in their pockets. Have students write on their T-shirts what kind of good luck they would like to have that day.

See a penny,
Pick it up,
All the day
You'll have good luck

I hope we win the game.

LUCKY CHARMS® SORTING

Give each student a handful of Lucky Charms cereal. Invite students to sort the marshmallow treats into separate piles. Have students use crayons or markers to graph how many of each shape they received. Total student results and record them on a class graph. Invite students to munch on their treats.

LOOK AT OUR LUCK!

90
80
70
60
50
40
30
20
10

MY LUCKY SHAMROCK

The shamrock is Ireland's national symbol, and it is a custom to wear one on St. Patrick's Day to show pride in being Irish. A shamrock with four leaves is supposed to bring the finder good luck and protection from harm. Have students use the Shamrock reproducible to write a story about finding a lucky four-leaf shamrock. Display the stories on a green construction-paper background.

POCKET

See a penny.
Pick it up.
All the day
You'll have good luck.

March © 1997 Creative Teaching Press

This is what I'm going to do with my shamrock _____

When I showed my shamrock to _____, he/she said _____

I found my shamrock _____

My shamrock brought me good luck when _____

FIRST DAY OF SPRING

March 20

Spring is filled with signs of new life—flowers blooming, birds chirping, and snow melting. Celebrating the new season will bring a spring to your students' steps and a smile to their faces.

LITERATURE LINKS

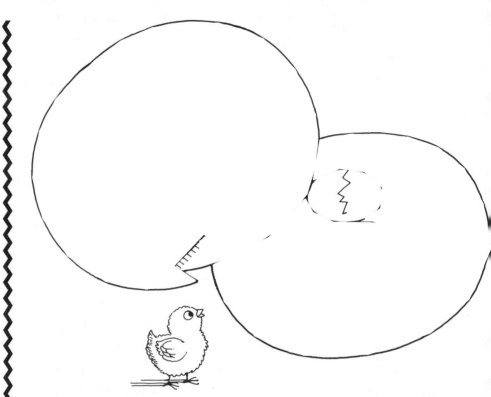

HATCHING CHICKS

Read aloud *Make Way for Ducklings*. Borrow an incubator and eggs from a chicken farm so students can observe hatching chicks. Have students record and illustrate on egg-shaped paper main events leading up to and following the eggs hatching. When chicks hatch, teach responsibility for little creatures. Bind students' pages into egg-shaped books. Return the chicks and incubator when the chicks are three weeks old.

MATERIALS

- ▲ incubator
- ▲ eggs (from chicken farm)
- ▲ *Make Way for Ducklings* by Robert McCloskey
- ▲ egg-shaped paper
- ▲ crayons or markers
- ▲ bookbinding materials

SPRINGTIME TREES

MATERIALS

▲ *Sky Tree* by Thomas Locker and Candace Christiansen
▲ construction paper
▲ paint/paintbrushes
▲ sponges
▲ index cards
▲ pencils or cotton swabs

Share *Sky Tree* with your class as an inspiration before students make their own paintings of springtime trees. Have students sponge-paint the top three-quarters of white construction paper with shades of blue for a sky and sponge-paint grass in shades of green on the bottom quarter. Invite students to dip the edges of an index card into different shades of green paint and press the painted edges onto the paper to create a grassy effect. When the background is dry, have each student paint a brown trunk and branches. Students can add pink and white blossoms to the grass and tree by dipping the flat end of a pencil, a cotton swab, or their fingers in paint and pressing them onto the paper.

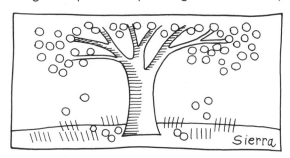

LITTLE LAMBS

MATERIALS

▲ yogurt cups
▲ glue
▲ cotton balls
▲ clothespins
▲ white and black paint/paintbrushes
▲ black pom-poms
▲ felt
▲ wiggly eyes

Have students cover yogurt cups with glue and cotton balls. Invite students to paint four clothespins white. When dry, have students paint the "squeeze" ends black. Have each student clip the four clothespins around the cup to form legs and glue on a black pom-pom head, two ears cut from felt, and wiggly eyes.

ROBIN REDBREAST

MATERIALS

▲ drawing paper
▲ crayons or pastels
▲ glue
▲ brown tissue paper
▲ scissors
▲ yellow and brown construction paper

The presence of robins are often a sign of spring. Have each student draw a circle and color the top half dark brown and the bottom half reddish-brown. Students can glue small, brown tissue-paper strips to the top half for texture. Have students cut out a yellow diamond-shaped beak and fold it in half before gluing on. Invite students to cut out and glue on construction-paper legs and eyes. Hang the robins from the ceiling to welcome spring!

MATERIALS

▲ blue construction paper
▲ black paint/paintbrushes
▲ hole-reinforcement rings or cotton balls and glue
▲ wiggly eyes
▲ ribbon

LITTLE LAMB CARDS

Have students fold blue construction paper in half widthwise. Ask students to paint the palm of one hand black, and have them make a handprint on the front of the card, outstretched fingers and thumb pointing down toward the bottom of the paper. (The fingers are the lamb's legs and the thumb is the head.) When the paint dries, have students stick on hole-reinforcement rings or glue on cotton balls to make the lamb's coat. Have each student add a wiggly eye to the thumb and glue a tiny bow to the neck. Invite students to write *Happy Spring from your Little Lamb* inside the card.

MATERIALS

▲ small pinecones
▲ yellow spray paint
▲ fiberfill or cotton balls
▲ pencil
▲ felt or construction paper scraps
▲ scissors
▲ glue
▲ margarine tubs
▲ Easter grass

BABY CHICKS

Spray-paint pinecones yellow and let dry. Invite students to wrap pinecones with fiberfill or cotton balls and use a pencil to poke the fluff between the pinecone scales. Have students cut wings, a beak, and eyes from felt or construction paper and glue them to the body. Invite students to fill margarine tubs with Easter grass and place their chicks inside.

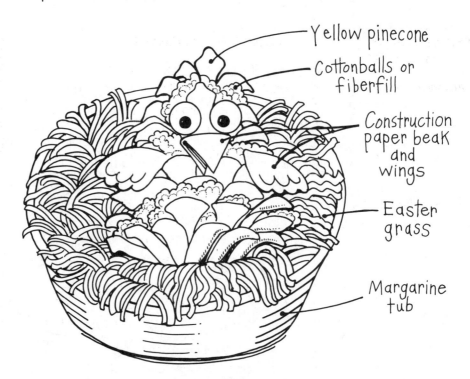

Yellow pinecone

Cottonballs or fiberfill

Construction paper beak and wings

Easter grass

Margarine tub

MIME DAY

March 22

Marcel Marceau, the French mime, was born on March 22, 1923. Save words on this quiet day by pantomiming whenever possible. If you must speak, use a French accent!

LITERATURE LINKS

Animal Action Alphabet: A Rhyme 'N' Mime by Karen Pandell, et al.

Shy Charles by Rosemary Wells

Sing Pierrot, Sing: A Picture Book in Mime by Tomie dePaola

MIRROR, MIRROR

Pair up students and assign one as leader and the other as follower. Invite students to stand across from their partner, put their hands out in front of them, and look at their partner's eyes. Ask the leaders to slowly move their hands and have the followers try to mirror the movements. After a few minutes, ask students to switch roles. Ask one pair of students to volunteer to do the activity while others watch. Tell the volunteers in a whisper who will be the leader and follower. Ask students to guess which student is the follower and which is the leader. If the volunteers are careful, the class won't be able to tell.

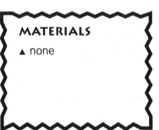

MATERIALS
▲ none

MATERIALS
▲ water-based paints/paintbrushes

FACE PAINTING

Ask students to wear black and white to school to dress like Marcel Marceau. Invite students to pair up to paint each other's faces with water-based paints. Demonstrate how to paint the background white and paint little designs in different colors. Warn students to keep the paint away from their eyes. Afterward, invite students to play Don't Say a Word.

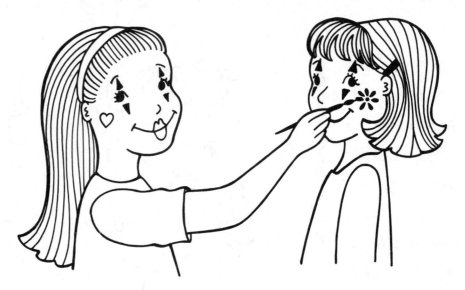

MATERIALS
▲ index cards
▲ Pantomime reproducible (page 81)
▲ glue

DON'T SAY A WORD!

Cut and paste each mime activity from the Pantomime reproducible onto separate index cards. Have each student select an index card, practice the pantomime at home, and present it in class the following day. Introduce students by announcing *Introducing (girl's first name) Marceau* or *Marcel (boy's last name)*. The student who first guesses the pantomime gets the next turn.

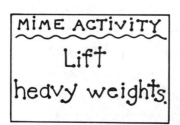

MIME ACTIVITY
Lift heavy weights.

PANTOMIME

1.	Change a baby's diaper.	16.	Milk a cow.
2.	Try to stifle a sneeze.	17.	Decorate a Christmas tree.
3.	Be a cat washing itself.	18.	Make a snowman.
4.	Take the trash out. It splits open and you fall in the mess.	19.	Try to keep yourself from coughing during a play.
5.	Be a tightrope walker.	20.	Paint your toenails.
6.	Lift heavy weights.	21.	Ride a bike for the first time.
7.	Pack a suitcase so full that you have trouble closing it.	22.	Try to get a baby to stop crying.
8.	Be a mouse sniffing cheese. Then get caught in a trap.	23.	Hammer a nail; then miss, and hit your finger.
9.	Open the refrigerator and drink milk out of a carton.	24.	Lose your glasses and then have trouble seeing.
10.	Wash your face and brush your teeth.	25.	Blame the trouble you are in on the person next to you.
11.	Fly a kite until it gets caught in a tree.	26.	Watch the lottery numbers on TV. Then you win!
12.	A big balloon on a windy day almost carries you away.	27.	Be a pirate having to walk the plank.
13.	Creep out of bed at night and sneak some cookies from the cookie jar.	28.	Secretly unwrap a present; then try to rewrap it without getting caught.
14.	Be a model posing for a picture in a magazine.	29.	Make a wish and blow out the candles on your birthday cake.
15.	Be a rock star.	30.	Walk right into a pile of mud.

COOKING DAY

March 23

Mix, bake, and cook to celebrate the birthday of the first cookbook author, Fannie Farmer. Young chefs will love making treats they can eat!

LITERATURE LINKS

Bunny Cakes
by Rosemary Wells

*A Cow, a Bee,
a Cookie, and Me*
by Meredith Hooper

The Giant Jam Sandwich
by John Vernon Lord

*The Magic School Bus
Gets Baked in a Cake*
by Joanna Cole

Mr. Cookie Baker
by Monica Wellington

My Grandma's Great
by Hannah Roche

One Hungry Cat
by Joanne Rocklin

Play with Your Food
by Joost Elffers

Too Many Babas
by Carolyn Croll

Walter the Baker by Eric Carle

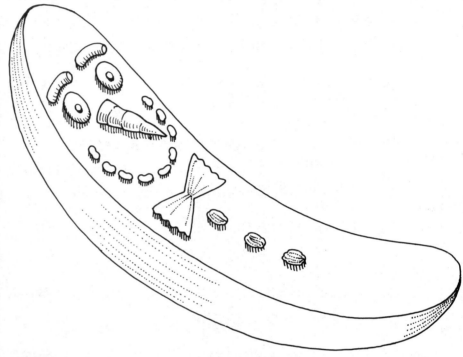

PLEASE PLAY WITH YOUR FOOD

Provide students with various foods for them to use in creating faces, monsters, or other delicious designs on paper plates. For example, peas, corn niblets, carrot rounds, black olives, beans, cereal, nuts, seeds, or raisins work well for eyes and noses; broccoli, cauliflower florets, grapes, fresh dill, parsley, and curly pasta work well for hair; thin celery sticks, carrot strips, and pretzel sticks work well for legs; and peanut butter, mayonnaise, cream cheese, jelly, yogurt, ketchup, mustard, pizza sauce, and honey work well for glue. Invite students to draw their healthy snack creations. Take photographs of students with their snacks and attach the photographs next to their drawings. Have students name their snacks and write their own recipes next to the photographs.

MATERIALS
▲ paper plates
▲ plastic knives
▲ crayons or markers
▲ instant camera/film
▲ food (as described)

CLASSY CHEF HATS

MATERIALS

▲ 4" x 18" (10 cm x 46 cm) white construction-paper strips

▲ hole punch

▲ white tissue paper

▲ glue

▲ brass fasteners

▲ rubber bands

▲ glue

Have students write *Chef* _____ on white construction-paper strips and hole-punch each end. Have students put a brass fastener in each hole and hook a rubber band around the fasteners to make a headband. Have each student fold a full-size white tissue-paper sheet in half lengthwise and glue the long sides together. Ask students to glue the tissue paper to the inside of the paper strip and glue the top of the hat closed. Invite students to wear their chef hats while cooking in class as well as when they help their parents cook at home.

SHAMROCKS ON A STICK

MATERIALS

▲ ¼ cup (50 ml) margarine

▲ electric skillet

▲ 40 large marshmallows

▲ 6 cups (1.5 l) crispy rice cereal

▲ green food coloring

▲ pan

▲ cooking spray

▲ shamrock cookie cutter

▲ craft sticks

Melt margarine in an electric skillet. Add marshmallows and stir until melted. Remove from heat and add crispy rice cereal. Invite students to take turns stirring. Add a few drops of green food coloring. Press mixture evenly into a pan coated with cooking spray. Cool completely. Cut into shamrock shapes using a cookie cutter and serve on craft sticks.

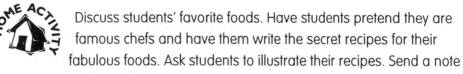

CLASS COOKBOOK

MATERIALS

▲ drawing paper

▲ crayons or markers

▲ bookbinding materials

Discuss students' favorite foods. Have students pretend they are famous chefs and have them write the secret recipes for their fabulous foods. Ask students to illustrate their recipes. Send a note home asking family members to write their versions of the same recipes their child wrote. Attach the two versions and photocopy each recipe so each student has one of each. Bind the recipes into individual cookbooks for students to take home and share with their families. Bind the originals into a class book.

Our Favorite Recipes

by Miss Tomita's 3rd graders

Chef Lorette

Mashed potatoes

First put potatoes in the blender.

Add whipped cream and yogurt.

Heat in a bowl.

SECRET RECIPE

Chef Jeff

My favorite food is peanut butter and banana sandwiches.

Put peanut butter on bread.

Add bananas. Eat!

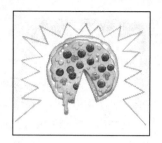

PIZZA DAY

Pizza ranks as one of the all-time favorite foods. Add some spice to March by celebrating Pizza Day with these perfect pizza projects.

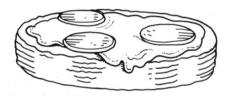

LITERATURE LINKS

The Berenstain Bears and the Sci-Fi Pizza
by Stan and Jan Berenstain

Curious George and the Pizza
by Margaret Rey

"Hi, Pizza Man!"
by Virginia Walter and Ponder Goembel

Hold the Anchovies!: A Book about Pizza
by Shelley Rotner and Julia P. Hellums

How Pizza Came to Our Town
by Dayal Khalsa

The King of Pizza: A Magical Story about the World's Favorite Food
by Sylvester Sanzari

The Pizza Book
by Stephen Krensky

Sam's Pizza: Your Pizza to Go
by David Pelham

PERFECT PIZZAS

Give each student a toasted English muffin half to use in building a pizza. Have students spread pizza sauce on the muffins with craft sticks. Invite students to sprinkle on grated cheese and pepperoni. Broil two muffins at a time in a toaster oven until the cheese melts. Challenge students to divide their pizzas into different fractional pieces. Enjoy!

MATERIALS
▲ toaster oven
▲ toasted English muffins
▲ pizza sauce
▲ craft sticks
▲ grated cheese
▲ pepperoni
▲ plastic knives

MATERIALS

▲ 4" (10 cm) construction-paper circles
▲ crayons or markers
▲ large butcher-paper circle
▲ glue
▲ sentence strips

ON MY PIZZA . . .

Ask students what their favorite pizza toppings are. Divide a butcher-paper circle into as many sections as necessary—pepperoni, cheese, sausage, olive, mushroom, and Canadian bacon and pineapple. Have each student draw a picture of a favorite topping on construction-paper circles and glue it to the correct section of the graph. Write student observations about the graph on sentence strips and attach them around the graph.

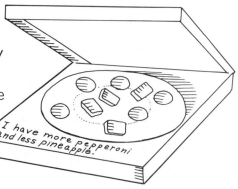

Sausage was least popular.

We like pepperoni best.

More people like olives than mushrooms.

MATERIALS

▲ scissors
▲ felt or construction-paper
▲ paper plates
▲ pizza box

TOPPINGS GALORE

Cut out colorful "pizza toppings" such as pepperoni, pineapple, tomato, mushroom, olive, and sausage from felt or construction paper for students to use as math manipulatives. Have students sort the toppings and arrange them on a paper-plate "pizza." Create story problems your class can illustrate using the toppings. For example, *My pizza has five olives and two pepperoni slices. How many toppings do I have?* or *My pizza has ten topping pieces. It has two sausage pieces and the rest are pineapple. How many pineapple pieces do I have?* Store the paper plates and toppings in a pizza box and place in a learning center.

I have more pepperoni and less pineapple.

MATERIALS

▲ tagboard circles
▲ art supplies (crayons, markers, construction paper, felt scraps)
▲ pizza box
▲ stapler
▲ resealable plastic bags
▲ glue
▲ scissors

PIZZA FRACTIONS

HOME ACTIVITY

Divide your class into five groups. Have each group use art supplies to decorate a tagboard circle to make a different kind of pizza. Glue one blank tagboard circle to the inside bottom of the pizza box. Divide each of the five student pizzas into different fractional pieces (half, thirds, fourths, sixths, and eighths) and laminate. Put pizza pieces in resealable plastic bags and place them in the pizza box. Each day, send the box home with a student and ask him or her to write story problems and place them in the bags with the pizza pieces for other students to try.

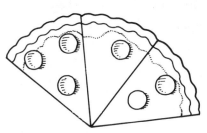

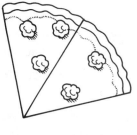

DOCTORS' DAY

March 30

Honor physicians who keep us healthy and help us when we are ill. Invite students to be doctors today. Have them learn about germs and write their own prescriptions for the common cold.

LITERATURE LINKS
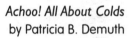

Achoo! All About Colds
by Patricia B. Demuth

A Big Operation
by Richard Scarry

Curious George Goes to the Hospital
by Margaret and H.A. Rey

Cuts, Breaks, Bruises, and Burns: How the Body Heals
by Joanna Cole

Dinosaurs Alive and Well! A Guide to Good Health
by Laurie Krasney Brown

Germs Make Me Sick!
by Melvin Berger

Healthy Me
by Angela Royston

The Hospital Scares Me
by Paula Z. Hogan

HEAR THE BEAT

Explain why doctors use stethoscopes to listen to our hearts. Ask each student to stretch a balloon over the top of a cut plastic bottle and tape it securely in place. Have students cut a hole in the tip of the balloons and push rubber tubing through the balloon into the mouth of the bottle. Ask students to place the wide end of their "stethoscopes" to the partner's chest and listen through the tube at the other end. Extend learning by having students listen to breathing patterns through the stethoscopes. Invite them to compare breathing patterns to heartbeats. Have students listen for heartbeats before and after running.

MATERIALS
▲ long balloons
▲ 2-liter plastic bottles (bottom two-thirds cut off)
▲ tape
▲ rubber tubing

ALL ABOUT GERMS

Have each student trim the edges of the All about Germs reproducible and fold it on the dotted lines to make a booklet. Read the booklet with students so they can learn about how to prevent germs from making them sick. Have students work in small groups to illustrate on poster board one of the healthy habits from the last page of the booklet. Display posters around the school or classroom. Ask students to take the booklets home to read with their family members.

CREATIVE COLD CURES

Discuss with students how there is no cure for the common cold. Invite students to pretend they are doctors who have discovered the cure. Have students write on the Clipboard reproducible their prescriptions for the common cold. Invite students to share their remedies with the class.

ALL ABOUT GERMS

Page 3

Viruses are even tinier. They look like this:

There are many kinds of germs, but two kinds that can make us sick are bacteria and viruses. Bacteria look like this:

Page 2

Germs are very tiny living beings. They are so tiny, you cannot see them without a microscope. A microscope makes germs look much bigger. One thousand germs could fit on a pencil point.

Healthy Habits

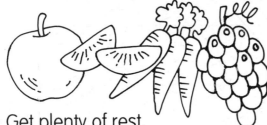

- Get plenty of rest.
- Exercise three times a week.
- Eat healthy foods.
- Cover your mouth and nose when you sneeze or cough.
- Wash your hands with soap and warm water after you go to the bathroom.
- Wash your hands before you eat.

Page 4

All about Germs

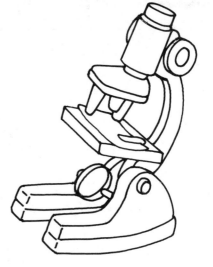

_____

Name

Page 1

March © 1997 Creative Teaching Press

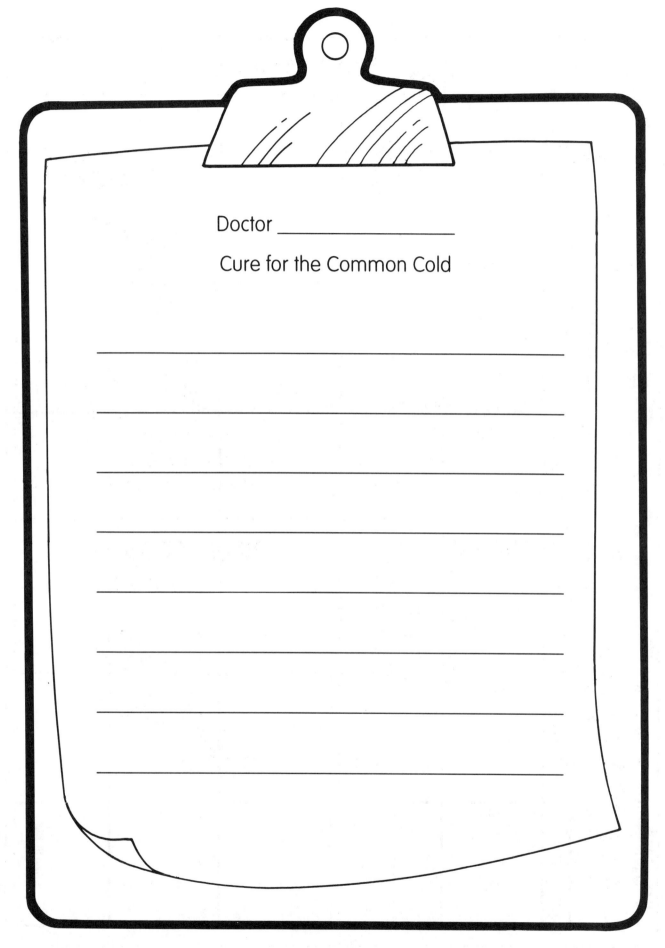

Doctor _____

Cure for the Common Cold

_____

_____

_____

_____

_____

_____

_____

MARCH

March Calendar

SUNDAY	MONDAY	TUESDAY	WEDNESDAY	THURSDAY	FRIDAY	SATURDAY

Shamrock Border

March © 1997 Creative Teaching Press

March Newsletter

Clip Art